# DEFINING
### AND
# DESCRIBING

## Marilyn M. Toomey

Illustrated by Kevin M. Newman

CIRCUIT PUBLICATIONS

Marblehead, MA

Copyright ©1991
by Circuit Publications
PO Box 1201
Marblehead, Mass. 01945
All rights reserved.

00 99 98 97 96 TS 6 5

ISBN: 0-923573-14-3

Printed in the United States of America on recycled paper.

# Table of Contents

# Preface

Defining and describing occur routinely in many language arts programs. A student's early encounters with definitions probably leads to using a dictionary or glossary from which he or she might copy or prepare to retell the information. Descriptions often consist of simple statements plus words or phrases drawn out of a student by a teacher encouraging the student to "tell more about it." Such measures get the job done - the student produces a definition or description, but, such experiences do not develop the student's ability to define or describe other things. If this student is asked to define or describe something in another setting, he or she might well look for a dictionary or for an encouraging teacher for help even if he or she knows something about the object.

Students would be better equipped to handle these language tasks if they had within their repertoire a format with which to construct a definition or description. This book was designed to help teach such formats. Using discourse between two cartoon-like characters, patterns or structures for defining and describing are identified. Students learn that it is important to use a suitable format to deliver information so that communication flows smoothly.

Definitions and descriptions are composed of names of objects, words denoting various classifications, and attributes or characteristics. To help you implement your instruction, this book contains such words - hundreds of them! Using these words, and a bit of creativity, thousands of definitions and descriptions can be constructed.

The purpose of this book is to provide you with ideas and substance for helping students develop the important techniques of defining and describing. Twenty-plus years of working to enhance students' language ability has taught me that there's no easy way to develop such skills, but, good educational products help! I hope you find this book to be such a product.

# Introduction

*Defining and Describing* suggests formats or structure in which to construct definitions and descriptions as well as vocabulary with which to generate definitions and descriptions. This book follows a loose story line where a child, Mazey, from another planet, comes to Earth in search of information about our planet. Through dialogue with Charles, a child from Earth, patterns for constructing definitions and descriptions are developed. Subsequently, dozens of pages of words arranged according to classification or descriptive characteristics are presented. The suggested patterns plus vocabulary and practice pages should help students create countless definitions and descriptions.

In order for comfortable, fluent communication to occur, speakers (or writers) clearly present information so that listeners (or readers) easily receive it. The message must consist of appropriate vocabulary and syntax to clearly identify the contents. But, to complete the communication tasks, presenters must deliver information in a manner compatible with receivers' expectations. In formatting a message a presenter responds to cues from the receiver and the environment. The presenter knows what the listener is expecting and this knowledge directs the preparation of the message. When a presenter selects a mode of presentation corresponding to the anticipated mode of interception, communication flows smoothly. Otherwise communication breaks down.

Think of this. What if you asked someone to define a peach pie because you wanted to know what a peach pie was. Suppose, then, that the other person started saying something like, "Let me tell you how my grandmother makes one. First she gets some..." This extraneous information not only does not tell you what a peach pie is, but interferes with the mechanism which you have set up to receive the definition. The best case scenario would be for you to recognize that the wrong presentation mode had been selected and reiterate that you need to know *what* a peach pie is, not *how* to make one. The speaker would then respond by reformatting the message. In this situation, much of the same vocabulary and syntax applied for a definition of or an explanation of how to make a peach pie. Yet there was a breakdown in communicating because the speaker failed to consider your needs as a listener.

The tendency to use particular semantic configurations to meet certain communication goals is a skill which develops as a child's language system matures. Children observe competent language users arrange words in certain patterns depending on the type of message. As children's language systems develop they learn to respond to cues from the environment and from the persons who will receive the message. Patterns or structures in which to arrange information become part of a child's language system just as do vocabulary and the rules of syntax.

When a student is asked to define or describe the cues are simple and straightforward - the word *define* or *describe* is the cue that directs the student to prepare his or her message in the format of a definition or a description. The elementary student should be developing or should have developed the ability to tailor messages to meet specific communication goals. He or she should also have a store of vocabulary and knowledge of the rules of syntax sufficient to define and describe objects. Learning to utilize these abilities in response to the cues, *define* and *describe*, will make many language arts assignments more approachable. Sometimes we must learn to manage things that we own in order to make life easier - this also applies to language skills.

Students with language deficits likely need help learning the association between verbal/situational cues and proper presentation modes. Often these students fail to observe and internalize such communication techniques.

In *Defining and Describing* Mazey tells Charles how she receives and processes information (p.7). This leads to the establishment of a pattern for defining. First, the name of the object being defined, is stated. Second, the category or class in which the object belongs is named. Then some characteristics of this particular object which make it unique among others in its class are given.

A (NAME) is a (CLASSIFICATION) (CHARACTERISTICS).

This format is generally recognized as the best way to convey a definition. Researchers have observed children to follow a somewhat predictable pattern in developing this skill. Between ages five and ten years children's definitions evolve from simple statements consisting of words denoting obvious physical properties to statements including the name of the object being defined and the name of its classification followed by progressively more of its unique characteristics.

The most significant event in this process is the tendency to name the classification or category of the subject of the definition. Classifying things according to similarities is a fundamental cognitive ability and a significant function in the acquisition of knowledge. As members of a category are bound by similar traits, the category itself can be identified by these traits. When an unfamiliar object is encountered one recognizes characteristics with which he or she is familiar, and proceeds to classify this novel entity according to these known traits. Then this unfamiliar object (or creature) in turn, takes on the general characteristics of the class.

If a child who had never seen a motorcycle before saw someone riding by on a motorcycle she would assign this novel object, *motorcycle*, to the class, *motor vehicle* on the basis of its sound and apparent purpose. At that moment the motorcycle would take on the properties of motor vehicles (a steering mechanism, exhaust fumes, etc.). Through the process of classification the child has broadened her concept of *motor vehicle* to include motorcycle, and has begun to develop her concept of *motorcycle* to include characteristics which belong to motor vehicles in general (even though she did not yet experienced these characteristics as they pertain to motorcycles).

Receiving or presenting a definition, a person utilizes the process of classification to associate new information with something familiar. A receiver, hearing or reading the name of a category, instantly classifies this new item with others like it. A presenter accommodates this process by identifying the category of the novel object. Time spent developing and utilizing the process of classification is an investment in a child's collection of knowledge far beyond learning how to define. For this reason, vocabulary is organized according to classification of objects and ideas. Each group of objects and descriptive characteristics is presented on an illustrated page followed by a support page encouraging students to complete an activity (or activities) while focusing on a particular concept (foods, animals, words denoting color, distance, etc.)

By contrast, a description is constructed more loosely than a definition. After focusing on defining objects using a proper format, Mazey uses this same format to tell Charles about a particular dog (p. 106). Here, Charles points out that, since he already knows what a dog is, she need not tell him the name of its classification. When someone describes something his or her job is to create a sensory image of the object in the mind of the listener or reader by stating characteristics or attributes of this object. Assuming a receiver knows the category to which the subject of a description belongs, and, thus has some general knowledge of such objects, the format for a description is simply:

**NAME OF OBJECT + CHARACTERISTICS WHICH MAKE THIS OBJECT UNIQUE AMONG MEMBERS OF ITS CLASS**

The final portion of the book consists of guidelines, ideas, and practice material for students to construct definitions and descriptions. As you can see, the techniques and substance which go into constructing definitions and descriptions are quite remarkable. I hope that this book proves to be a valuable resource as you teach these important language functions.

## DEFINING AND DESCRIBING...
## I DO IT ALL THE TIME:

### DEFINING...

*WORDS ABOUT SPORTS*

*DIFFERENT FOODS THAT I TRY*

*WORDS ON SCIENCE TESTS*

*TOOLS THAT I USE*

### DESCRIBING...

*CLOTHES THAT MY
FRIENDS WEAR*

*PLACES I GO*

*ANIMALS I SEE
IN THE PARK...*

*...AND A LOT MORE!*

**BUT,** *I NEVER THOUGHT I'D BE DEFINING AND DESCRIBING JUST ABOUT* **EVERYTHING,** *UNTIL ONE DAY...*

*I WAS CUTTING THROUGH A PARKING LOT ON MY WAY TO THE STORE, WHEN ALL OF A SUDDEN...*

NOT EXACTLY. MY INFORMATION INPUT CENTER CAN NOT PROCESS YOUR DEFINITION OF A PARKING LOT.

GEE, I DEFINE THINGS ALL THE TIME, BUT I'M HAVING TROUBLE TELLING YOU ABOUT A PARKING LOT.

WAIT, I'LL HELP YOU. MY INFORMATION INPUT CENTER IS MADE UP OF SECTIONS. THERE'S A SECTION FOR EACH GROUP OF THINGS THAT I THINK ABOUT.

WHEN I SEE OR HEAR SOMETHING NEW, MY INFORMATION TRANSMITTER SENDS IT TO THE RIGHT SECTION WHERE I KEEP IT WHILE I THINK ABOUT IT AND LEARN MORE ABOUT IT.

OF COURSE!

**CLASSIFICATIONS!**

*THAT'S WHAT I DO WHEN I* **DEFINE..** *IF I TELL YOU THE NAME OF THE CATEGORY OF SOMETHING, THAT'LL HELP YOU KNOW WHAT IT IS. A PARKING LOT IS A* **PLACE..** *A PLACE FOR PARKING CARS... IT'S BIG, FLAT AND MADE OF DIRT OR STONE OR BLACKTOP.*

*OKAY! NOW I KNOW WHAT A PARKING LOT IS. CAN YOU TELL ME ABOUT SOME OTHER THINGS HERE ON EARTH? I WANT THIS TO BE THE BEST SOCIAL STUDIES PROJECT EVER!*

*SURE THING! FIRST I'LL TELL YOU HOW WE CLASSIFY THINGS - HOW WE ORGANIZE THINGS IN GROUPS SO WE CAN LEARN. THERE ARE SO MANY!*

*THERE ARE...*

| | | |
|---|---|---|
| FAMILY MEMBERS | BUILDINGS | THINGS TO EAT FOR BREAKFAST |
| FRIENDS | CLOTHES | |
| TEACHERS | UNIFORMS | DRINKS |
| GAMES | TOYS | SNACKS |
| PETS | DISHES | PIZZA TOPPINGS |
| CARS | BOATS | STORIES |
| COSTUMES | FURNITURE | THINGS TO EAT FOR LUNCH |

*AND MORE...*

*JUST ABOUT EVERYTHING IS CLASSIFIED WITH OTHER THINGS LIKE IT.*

*Defining and Describing*

HERE ARE SOME IMPORTANT **CLASSIFICATIONS** OR GROUPS OF THINGS HERE ON EARTH. THERE ARE LOTS OF THINGS IN EACH OF THESE GROUPS... ARE YOU READY?

READY !

places

buildings

animals

foods

clothing

vehicles

jobs and careers

tools

sports

entertainment

useful things

# Places

airport
baseball field
beach
bog
bridge
bus stop
campground
campus
canyon
cave
cemetery
city
cliff
continent
country
country club
county
crosswalk

desert
driveway
dunes
fair ground
farm
field
football field
forest
golf course
grassland
grove
harbor
highway
hill
island
jungle
kennel
marsh

meadow
mesa
mountain
neighborhood
oasis
orchard
park
parking lot
pasture
peninsula
plane
planet
playground
port
prairie
race track
reservation
resort

road
shopping mall
shore
solar system
stadium
state
street
subdivision
suburb
swamp
tennis court
town
train station
tundra
tunnel
valley
village
zoo

*Defining and Describing*

List some of the **places** that fit
into each of these categories:

wet places

_____

_____

_____

grassy places

_____

_____

_____

places for cars and trucks

_____

_____

_____

places where there should be no cars

_____

_____

_____

places to go on vacation

_____

_____

_____

places to have fun close to home

_____

_____

_____

places with many buildings

_____

_____

_____

places with no buildings

_____

_____

_____

What are some of your favorite places?  Why is each so special?

# Buildings

airplane hanger
apartment building
bank
barn
boat house
broadcast studio
cafe'
capitol building
car wash
castle
cathedral
church
city hall
club house
concert hall
condominium
control tower
convention center
cottage
court house
department store
dormitory
exhibition center
factory
fire station
greenhouse
gymnasium
hospital
hotel
house
library
lighthouse

log cabin
mansion
medical building
meeting hall
mill
mosque
motel
movie theater
nursing home
observatory
office building
palace
parking garage
police station
post office
prison
restaurant
school
service garage
shop
silo
sky scraper
sports arena
stable
supermarket
synagogue
theater
tool shed
town house
train depot
windmill

*Defining and Describing*

List some of the **buildings** that fit into each of these categories:

buildings where people live

_____

_____

_____

buildings where people work

_____

_____

buildings found in a town or city

_____

_____

_____

buildings you would probably *not* find in a town or city

_____

_____

_____

Which buildings would you associate with the following?

growing, selling or serving food

_____

_____

_____

gatherings of large numbers of people

_____

_____

_____

transportation

_____

_____

religions

_____

_____

entertainment

_____

_____

operations of local, state or national government

_____

_____

# Animals

beaver
chipmunk
deer
dog
fox
gerbil
goat
ground hog
opossum
rabbit
raccoon
sheep
skunk

ant
bumble bee
cicada
cockroach
cricket
dragon fly
earwig
fire fly
fly
frog
grasshopper
praying mantis
spider
termite
toad
walking stick

canary
crane
duck
eagle
goose
heron
ostrich
peacock
pelican
penguin
sand piper
sea gull
stork
swan
vulture

aardvark
bear
camel
cat
cow
coyote
giraffe
hippopotamus
horse
kangaroo
lion
llama
monkey
moose
rhinoceros
seal
tiger

buzzard
chicken
cuckoo
dove
falcon
finch
osprey
parakeet
partridge
pheasant
pigeon
quail
robin
rooster
swallow
swift
toucan

antelope
armadillo
bat
bear
camel
cheetah
dog
elephant
jaguar
sea lion
leopard
otter
porcupine
puma
weasel
zebra

barracuda
bass
catfish
cod
dolphin
electric eel
herring
jellyfish
mackerel
perch
sailfish
salmon
sea horse
shark
stingray
swordfish
trout
tuna

alligator
boa constrictor
cobra
crocodile
garter snake
lizard
python
rattlesnake
salamander
tortoise
turtle
viper
water moccasin

*Defining and Describing*

There are many ways of grouping **animals** together.  List some animals that fit into each of these categories.

animals that live in a forest

_____

_____

_____

_____

farm animals

animals that would not be pets

_____

_____

_____

_____

_____

_____

animals that might be pets

animals that move slowly

_____

_____

_____

_____

_____

_____

animals that move quickly

animals that eat other animals

_____

_____

_____

_____

_____

_____

animals that eat plants

_____

_____

_____

Find the names of **animals** in the box at the left.

```
O N E I R P H A I Z E B R A
T S F O X J B T O F M Y Z R
T R P C I G E R B I L S H M
E F M X O R A A I O E E H A
R X G W E G V S P J O L K D
A Y I G H N E S K U P G J I
A A R D V A R K F C A M E L
T H A K O D L R I G R D K O
D R F B M O O S E E D O G Q
W L F S P O D E R P M O N
W B E A R Y C A T K F T A S O V M E I S P D J
S O M E I F N L S P M F T R O U T S L G Y N E
```

Find the **fish** in the box on the right.

```
C B V W P D O R M D I X L
A S H S T I N G R A Y R L
T U N A D U I I Q T N D Y
F J K L D R T N W P W S F
I H P M A C K E R E L X I
S B Z O B N H J Y R F K S
H A D N G P C J M C J G H
D S A B H D O L P H I N E
R G H D S O R M S N
```

```
R O O S T E R M G O O S E
D K O W S P E M C S S O N R
P F P A R A K E E T J G D C
E D J N D B J G V R S S H F
L S O M U N D E D I S F T I
I S V T T S F A L C O N H N
C D D B O D G G O H P L E C
A S J Q U A I L D U H D S H
N D B Y C D J E B R D B Y J
D P M T A D P M V M T O D W
X F C A N A R Y Z K D O V E
```

Find the **birds** in the box on the left.

*Defining and Describing*

# Foods

almonds
apple
apricot
asparagus
bacon
bagels
banana
beans
beet
biscuit
blueberries
bologna
bread
broccoli
brussels sprouts
butter
cabbage
cake
candy
canteloup
carrots
cauliflower
celery
cereal
cheese
cheese puffs
cherry
chicken
chocolate sauce
cookies
corn chips
couscous
crackers
croissants
cucumber
duck

eggs
fish
French toast
fried clams
grapefruit
grapes
ham
hamburgers
ice cream
jelly
lemon
lettuce
lime
lobster

mango
milk
muffins
mushroom
nectarine
okra
onion
orange
pancakes
papaya
pasta
pastrami

peach
peanut butter
pear
pepperoni
peppers
pineapple
pita bread
plum
popcorn
potato
potato chips
pretzels
pumpkin
radish
raisins
rhubarb
ribs
rice
roast beef
salami
sausage
spinach
squash
steak
strawberries
sugar
syrup
tangerine
tortillas
turkey
turnips
waffles
walnuts
watermelon
whipping cream
yogurt

There are many ways of grouping **foods** together.  List some foods that fit into each of *these* groups.

Foods that should be cold

_____

_____

_____

_____

Foods that come in boxes

_____

_____

_____

_____

Picnic foods

_____

_____

_____

Things for sandwiches

_____

_____

_____

Breakfast foods

_____

_____

_____

_____

Foods that are round

_____

_____

_____

_____

Snack foods

_____

_____

_____

Foods that must be cooked

_____

_____

_____

Foods that are sweet

_____

_____

_____

_____

Foods that are crunchy

_____

_____

_____

_____

*Defining and Describing*

Nutritionists tell us that we should eat a balanced diet. This means that, each day, we should eat some **foods** from each of the four basic food groups, *meats, fruits and vegetables, dairy products*, and *grains* or foods made from grains like bread and cereal. Listed below are some of the foods from each of these food groups. Unscramble the words.

**Meats**

mha_____

shif_____

geasuas_____

taenup retubt_____

ketruy_____

conab_____

storbel_____

breguhmar_____

knicehc_____

kpor pohc_____

**Fruits and Vegetables**

arep_____

pealp_____

nooni_____

tootap_____

roak_____

reeppp_____

reychr_____

telectu_____

torrca_____

mlup_____

**Bread and Cereal**

bdrea_____

eack_____

ccerkar_____

koieco_____

spaat_____

finmuf_____

glabe_____

suitcbi_____

flefaw_____

lecrae_____

**Dairy Products**

terbut_____

macre_____

cie recam_____

grtyou_____

klim_____

sehece_____

Some foods are combined to make interesting things to eat.  List some **ingredients** that help make up each of these dishes.

| Tossed Salad | Pizza | Fruit Salad | Vegetable Soup |
|---|---|---|---|
| _____ | _____ | _____ | _____ |
| _____ | _____ | _____ | _____ |
| _____ | _____ | _____ | _____ |

| Banana Split | Beef Stew | Chow Mein |
|---|---|---|
| _____ | _____ | _____ |
| _____ | _____ | _____ |
| _____ | _____ | _____ |

Look at these lists of ingredients.  Can you guess what food contains all of the ingredients in each list?  Unscramble the words below and find the right food.

| hiilc | lcoe wasl | keac | tmea labls |
|---|---|---|---|
| paple iep | yer drbea | brindgeager | carmacion & sheece |

| _____ | _____ | _____ | _____ |
|---|---|---|---|
| yeast | sugar | ground meat | flour & shortening |
| sugar | butter | chopped onions | sugar & eggs |
| shortening | flour | tomato sauce | ginger |
| water | eggs & milk | chili powder | cinnamon |
| rye flour | baking powder | green peppers | baking soda |
| caraway seeds | vanilla | kidney beans | molasses |

| _____ | _____ | _____ | _____ |
|---|---|---|---|
| ground meat | cooked macaroni | flour | shredded cabbage |
| bread crumbs | milk | shortening | chopped onion |
| chipped onion | butter | water | grated carrots |
| garlic | salt | sliced apples | mayonnaise |
| salt | pepper | sugar | vinegar & sugar |
| egg | grated cheese | cinnamon | salt & pepper |

*Defining and Describing*

# Clothes

apron
belt
blazer
bloomers
blouse
boots
bow tie
cap
cape
cardigan
coat
cummerbund
dress
ear muffs
formal
gloves
gown
hat
jacket
jeans
jersey
jump suit
kimono
knickers
leotard
mini skirt
mittens
moccasins
muffler
negligee
overalls
pajamas
pants
panty hose
parka

pinafore
poncho
rain coat
robe
sandals
sarong
sash
scarf
shawl
shoes
shorts
ski pants
skirt
slacks
slicker
slippers
sneakers
socks
sport coat
stockings
suit
suspenders
sweat band
sweat pants
sweat shirt
sweater
swim suit
T-shirt
tie
tunic
tuxedo
uniform
veil
vest
wind breaker

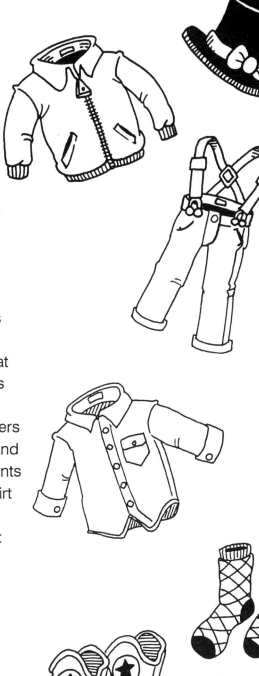

List some things to wear that fit into each of these categories.

Things that keep us warm
in cold weather

_____

_____

_____

Things that help keep us cool
in warm weather

_____

_____

_____

Things that are casual

_____

_____

_____

Things that are for dress-up

_____

_____

_____

Some **clothes** are associated with particular nationalities or cultures.  Draw a line from each item of clothing to the correct nationality or culture.

| | |
|---|---|
| sombrero | English |
| kilt | French |
| wooden shoes | Mexican |
| sari | Scottish |
| turban | Hawaiian |
| blue jeans | Jewish |
| derby (hat) | Dutch |
| beret | American |
| kimono | Moslem |
| grass skirt | Japanese |
| suit of armor | German |
| lederhosen | Medieval European |
| yarmulke | Indian |

*Defining and Describing*

# Vehicles

racing car
raft
recreation vehicles
row boat
sail boat
sedan
shopping cart
skateboard
snow mobile
space shuttle
speed boat
sports car
stage coach
station wagon
submarine
subway
surf board
taxi cab
tow truck
tractor
trailer
tram
tricycle
trolley car
tug boat
unicycle
van
wagon
yacht

aircraft carrier
ambulance
baby stroller
backhoe
barge
battleship
bicycle
blimp
buggy
bulldozer
bus
canoe
cargo ship
cement mixer
convertible
crane
dingy
dump truck
ferry boat
fire engine
fork lift truck
freight train
glider
golf cart
helicopter
horse-drawn carriage
house boat

hydrofoil
jet plane
kayak
limousine
monorail
moped
motor boat
motor cycle
motor home
moving van
ocean liner
oil tanker
paddle wheel river boat
passenger train
pick-up truck
police car
propeller plane

*Defining and Describing*

List some **vehicles** that fit into each of these categories.

Vehicles with motors or engines

_____

_____

_____

_____

Vehicles with wheels

_____

_____

_____

_____

Vehicles that run on "person power"

_____

_____

_____

_____

Construction vehicles

_____

_____

_____

_____

Fun vehicles

_____

_____

_____

_____

Vehicles for traveling long distances

_____

_____

_____

_____

Emergency vehicles

_____

_____

_____

_____

Vehicles used in the city

_____

_____

_____

_____

*Defining and Describing*

# Jobs and Careers

accountant
architect
artist
astronaut
athlete
baker
banker
barber
beautician
brick layer
broadcaster
builder
bus driver
butcher
cabinet maker
carpenter
chef
clergy member
coach
congresswoman or man
council member
custodian
disc jockey
doctor
dry cleaner
electrician
engineer
farmer
fashion designer
fire fighter

fisherman
florist
forest ranger
glazer
governor
inventor
jeweler
judge
laboratory technician
lawyer
librarian
lifeguard

long distance operator
longshoreman
lumberjack
mail carrier
mayor
mechanic
naturalist
newspaper reporter
nurse
painter
paramedic
photographer

physical therapist
pilot
plasterer
plumber
police officer
potter
president
principal
rancher
repair person
roofer
sailor
scientist
secretary
senator
sheriff
shopkeeper
social worker
soldier
speech pathologist
tailor
taxidermist
teacher
telephone line worker
trash collector
upholsterer
veterinarian
waiter
writer
x-ray technician

List some of the **careers** of the people in each of these categories.

People who work in hospitals

_____

_____

_____

_____

People who are elected to their jobs

_____

_____

_____

_____

People who build houses

_____

_____

_____

People who work to bring us our food

_____

_____

_____

Look at the list of **jobs**.  Who would be best qualified to perform each?

give a manicure_____

transfer goods
from a ship_____

vaccinate a dog_____

rewire an old house_____

prepare a tax return_____

cut glass for a window_____

explore outer space_____

build a fireplace_____

repair a watch_____

conduct a
religious service_____

repair a leaky faucet_____

prevent someone
from drowning_____

design a safe car_____

make a new law_____

keep books in order_____

make a new suit_____

deliver the mail_____

compete in
the Olympics_____

hire a new teacher_____

represent someone
accused of a crime_____

*Defining and Describing*

# Tools

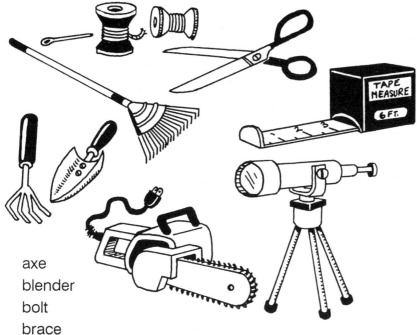

sauce pan
scale
scissors
scraper
screw
screw driver
shovel
skillet
soldering gun
spatula
spoon
sprayer
tape measure
telescope
test tube
thimble
thread
tiller
torch
trowel
typewriter
vice
weeder
wheelbarrow
wrench

axe
blender
bolt
brace
calculator
chain saw
chisel
clamp
computer
drill
easel
food chopper
garden hoe
garden hose
grater
hack saw
hammer
hand saw
hedge clipper
iron
knife

ladder
lawn mower
mallet
measuring cup
microscope
nail
needle
paint brush
pencil
plane
pliers
posthole digger
pruning shears
rake
roller

List some **tools** that fit into each of these categories.

Tools made of metal

_____

_____

_____

_____

_____

Tools for measuring or analyzing

_____

_____

_____

_____

_____

Tools that are sharp

_____

_____

_____

_____

Tools with handles

_____

_____

_____

_____

Tools for putting things together

_____

_____

_____

Tools for taking things apart

_____

_____

_____

Tools that are associated with heat

_____        _____

_____        _____

*Defining and Describing*

Find a **tool** (or tools) that each worker listed below would use.
Solve the puzzle.

**ACROSS**

2. Writer
4. Plumber
5. Chef
7. Sculptor
9. Scientist
11. Chef
13. Painter
14. Farmer
15. Painter
16. Gardener
18. Chef
20. Tailor
21. Carpenter
22. Tailor
23. Chef
25. Chef
29. Painter
32. Gardener
34. Gardener
36. Gardener
37. Writer
39. Artist
40. Mechanic
41. Scientist
44. Carpenter
45. Carpenter

**DOWN**

1. Tailor
3. Accountant
6. Lumberjack
8. Carpenter
10. Chef
12. Painter
17. Carpenter
19. Gardener
24. Mechanic
26. Farmer
27. Tailor
28. Carpenter
30. Mechanic
31. Gardener
33. Tailor
35. Scientist
38. Gardener
40. Chef
42. Chef
43. Carpenter

© Circuit Publications

*Defining and Describing*

Tools **29**

# Sports

field hockey
figure skating
fishing
football
golf
gymnastics
handball
hang gliding
hot air balloon racing
hunting
ice hockey
jai alai
lacrosse
ping pong
polo
racquetball

archery
auto racing
badminton
baseball
basketball
bike racing
bobsleding
bowling
boxing
canoeing
cricket
croquet
cycling
diving
fencing

rodeo riding
rowing
rugby
sailing
skiing
slalom
soccer
speed skating
squash
swimming
tennis
track
**volleyball**
wind surfing
wrestling

*Defining and Describing*

List some **sports** that fit into each of these categories.

team sports

_____

_____

_____

individual sports

_____

_____

_____

winter sports

_____

_____

_____

indoor sports

_____

_____

_____

outdoor sports

_____

_____

_____

sports involving a ball

_____

_____

_____

sports involving a racquet

_____

_____

_____

water sports

_____

_____

_____

contact sports (sports in which players might physically contact each other during play)

_____

_____

_____

_____

_____

_____

Find something used in each of the **sports** listed below. Solve the puzzle.

## ACROSS

1. Archery
4. Ping Pong
5. Golf
8. Rodeo
9. Swimming
11. Track
14. Balloon Racing
15. Football
16. Baseball
17. Soccer
20. Skiing
22. Fencing
24. Bobsledding
25. Figure Skating
26. Sailing

## DOWN

1. Basketball
2. Tennis
3. Volleyball
5. Auto Racing
6. Fishing
7. Raquetball
10. Bowling
12. Rowing
13. Cycling
16. Diving
18. Boxing
19. Polo
21. Hockey
23. Gymnastics

*Defining and Describing*

# Entertainment

## ENTERTAINERS
actor
ballerina
clown
disc jockey
ice skater
juggler
master of ceremonies
mime
musician
puppeteer
singer
tap dancer
tight rope walker
ventriloquist

## MUSIC
choral
classical
country-western
folk
jazz
pop
reggae
rock and roll

## MUSICAL INSTRUMENTS
banjo
cello
clarinet
cymbal
drum
flute
French horn
guitar
harmonica
harp
harpsichord
organ
piano
recorder
saxophone
tambourine
trombone
trumpet
tuba
violin
xylophone

## SPECIAL EVENTS
baseball game
basketball game
camping trip
carnival
circus
dance recital
fair
football game
half time show
hay ride
hockey game
ice show
music recital
parade
play
prom
rodeo
show music
square dance
symphony concert
TV show
variety show

Find something used by each of the **entertainers** below.
Solve the puzzle.

ACROSS

1. Director
2. Ice Skater
4. Singer
5. Musician
6. Ventriloquist
7. Juggler
8. Symphony conductor

DOWN

1. Actor
3. Clown
4. Puppeteer

Find the **musical instruments!**

| D | T | O | X | O | Y | C | D | P | I | Z | R | O | C | E | L | L | O | M | N | E | P |
| B | Y | B | H | W | O | G | X | D | O | S | Q | X | R | O | N | T | L | S | C | Y | R |
| U | H | A | R | P | W | U | J | R | T | A | E | C | L | A | R | I | N | E | T | P | W |
| L | Y | N | T | N | O | I | S | U | H | X | G | N | X | O | S | F | N | G | Y | T | S |
| T | Y | J | X | B | O | T | A | M | B | O | U | R | I | N | E | Q | U | B | Y | R | M |
| T | N | O | W | U | Y | A | B | N | V | P | W | S | G | H | F | Y | O | L | S | O | P |
| G | T | Q | O | G | X | R | T | H | M | H | A | R | M | O | N | I | C | A | P | M | C |
| L | U | S | F | E | E | N | S | D | L | O | V | N | S | O | W | N | V | O | F | B | N |
| X | B | O | E | L | S | M | C | N | S | N | S | N | D | O | E | P | I | A | N | O | W |
| O | A | G | F | L | U | T | E | E | R | E | C | O | R | D | E | R | I | U | N | N | T |
| T | N | S | O | E | A | S | D | H | T | O | R | U | S | L | T | R | U | M | P | E | T |
| T | N | O | W | F | X | Y | L | O | P | H | O | N | E | Q | J | O | R | G | A | N | W |

*Defining and Describing*

# Useful Things

## CONTAINERS
bag
basket
bottle
bowl
box
bucket
can
canteen
carton
cooler
cup
glass
jar
jug
pitcher
suitcase
tube
vase

## FASTENERS
buckle
button
clasp
latch
grippers
pin
snap
staple
tape
Velcro
zipper

## FUELS, something to burn in order to produce energy
butane
charcoal
coal
diesel oil
gasoline
kerosene
natural gas
oil
propane
wood

## UTENSILS, gadgets used in the kitchen
can opener
cheese slicer
egg beater
garlic press
grater
ladle
measuring cups
mixer
pizza cutter
potato peeler
rolling pin
spatula

## FURNITURE
bed
buffet
cabinet
chair
couch
desk
dresser
table

## SOURCES OF INFORMATION
advertisements
book
catalog
films
letters
magazine
newspaper
radio
television

## APPLIANCES
blender
clothes dryer
dishwasher
food processor
freezer
iron
microwave oven
refrigerator
stove
toaster
washer
water heater

Each of the words in this puzzle is **something useful** to us in our daily lives.
Solve the puzzle. The clues tell you into which category each of these items fit.

ACROSS
1. Fastener
3. Funiture
4. Container
6. Fuel
9. Sources of information
10. Fuel
11. Container
12. Sources of information
15. Furniture
18. Appliance
19. Sources of information
21. Sources of information
22. Fuel
24. Appliance
27. Furniture
32. Container
33. Appliance
35. Fuel
38. Fastener
41. Container
43. Furniture
44. Furniture
45. Container
47. Fastener
48. Container
49. Appliance

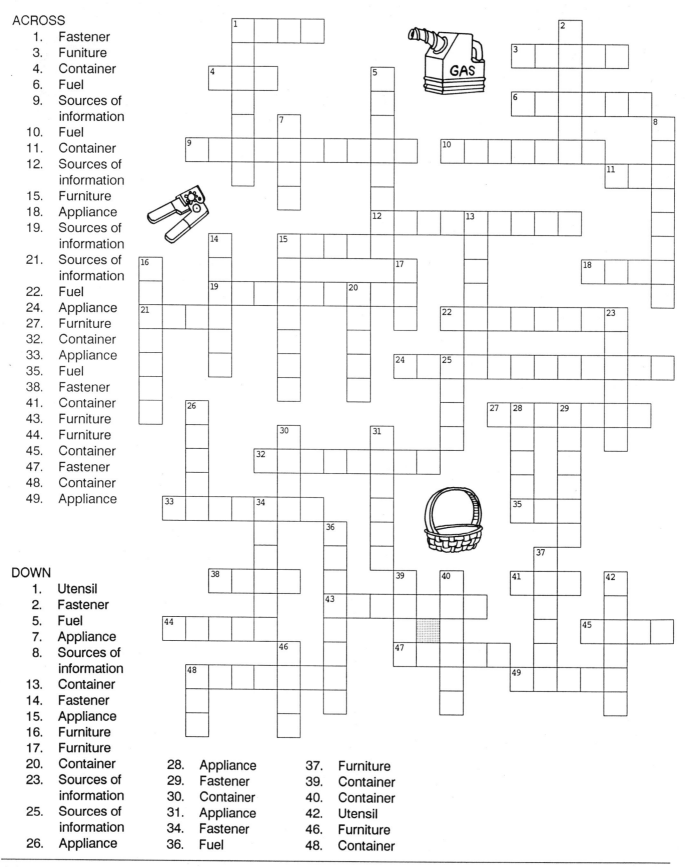

DOWN
1. Utensil
2. Fastener
5. Fuel
7. Appliance
8. Sources of information
13. Container
14. Fastener
15. Appliance
16. Furniture
17. Furniture
20. Container
23. Sources of information
25. Sources of information
26. Appliance
28. Appliance
29. Fastener
30. Container
31. Appliance
34. Fastener
36. Fuel
37. Furniture
39. Container
40. Container
42. Utensil
46. Furniture
48. Container

*Defining and Describing*

# Classifications Review

Can you match these items with their classifications?  Draw lines from items on the left to their classifications on the right.

barge

buckle

cheetah

chisel

kangaroo

clasp

helicopter

raft

latch

level

mackerel

van

pin

rake

staple

thimble

unicycle

Velcro

eagle

wrench

zebra

animal

vehicle

tool

fastener

# Classifications Review

Things are the same when they can be put into groups.  Name these categories.

■ Apples, oranges, and grapes are _____.

■ Shirts, pants, and swimsuits are _____.

■ Clasps, snaps, and buckles are _____.

■ Chairs, tables, and desks are _____.

■ A city, a meadow and a desert are _____.

■ A library, a factory, and a meeting hall are _____.

■ Fencing, boxing, and polo are _____.

■ A can opener, a spatula, and a rolling pin are _____.

■ Coal, oil, and natural gas are _____.

■ A saxophone, a cello, and a violin are _____.

■ A carton, a basket, and a jug are _____.

■ A hammer, a chisel, and a plow are _____.

*Defining and Describing*

# Classifications Review

Each of the lists below include three items that belong together because they are members of the same category. One of the items does not belong because it is not classified with the others. In the blanks write the names of items that belong together, the one that does not belong and its classification.

classifications:

| container | food | career | tool |
|---|---|---|---|
| vehicle | animal | sport | |

eggs
milk
cheese
frog

_____, _____ and _____ are foods.

_____ is not a food. It's an _____.

elephant
buffalo
yogurt
crocodile

_____, _____ and _____ are animals.

_____ is not an animal. It's a _____.

broadcasting
tractor
accounting
nursing

_____, _____ and _____ are careers.

_____ is not a career. It's a _____.

sport coat
shawl
basket
tuxedo

_____, _____ and _____ are clothes.

_____ is not clothing. It's a _____.

bagel
desk
dresser
sofa

_____, _____ and _____ are furniture.

_____ is not furniture. It's a _____.

torch
tractor
moving van
motorcycle

_____, _____ and _____ are vehicles.

_____ is not a vehicle. It's a _____.

skiing
soccer
polo
lumberjack

_____, _____ and _____ are sports.

_____ is not a sport. It's a _____.

tennis
sky scraper
library
greenhouse

_____, _____ and _____ are buildings.

_____ is not a building. It's a _____.

WHEN YOU DEFINE SOMETHING YOU NEED TO TELL WHAT CATEGORY IT BELONGS IN **AND ALSO** SOME THINGS ABOUT WHAT YOU'RE DEFINING THAT MAKE IT SPECIAL... ITS UNIQUE CHARACTERISTICS.

HERE'S HOW TO DEFINE SOMETHING:

- **First, say the name (the subject of your definition) that you're defining.**

- **Next, tell your listener the category into which the word fits.**

- **Finally, list the characteristics which make your subject special.**

LIKE THIS:

A ___name___ is a ___classification___ ___characteristics___ .

GOT IT! THAT SOUNDS LIKE QUITE A MANAGEABLE FORMULA; I'LL PROGRAM IT IN AT ONCE!

JUST ONE THING - WHAT ARE SOME OF THESE CHARACTERISTICS THAT MAKE THINGS SPECIAL? THERE MUST BE MANY, MANY DIFFERENT CHARACTERISTICS.

YOU'RE RIGHT.
THERE ARE HUNDREDS!

OH BOY! I'D BETTER RECHARGE MY INPUT RECEPTOR...
OKAY, I'M READY. TELL ME ABOUT THE CHARACTERISTICS THAT MAKE THINGS SPECIAL AND UNIQUE.

EVERY THING, EVERY ANIMAL, AND EVERY PERSON IN OUR WORLD IS UNIQUE AND VERY SPECIAL. HERE ARE SOME OF THE

# CHARACTERISTICS

OR TRAITS THAT MAKE PEOPLE, ANIMALS, OR THINGS SPECIAL.

I'M LISTENING !

| | |
|---|---|
| **Color** | color or combinations of colors |
| **Brightness** | degree of light or shadow |
| **Size** | how big or small something is in relation to some other thing |
| **Shape** | A particular shape is often associated with certain things. |
| **Texture** | the nature of a substance; how it is held together |
| **Touch** | how something feels to the touch |
| **Weight** | how heavy or light something is |
| **Material** | the product or products from which something is made |
| **Strength** | degree of power or force |
| **Taste** | the flavor of a substance |
| **Smell** | The scent associated with something |
| **Sound** | Unique noises or sounds associated with some objects |
| **Distance** | how far or near something is from a given point |
| **Value** | the price or worth of something |
| **Position** | how something is positioned in space when compared to other things |
| **Motion** | movement of an object or parts of an object |
| **Order** | how something is arranged |
| **Time** | relative age, historical period or temporal order |
| **Importance** | significance or stature |
| **Appearance** | how something looks to an observer |
| **Style** | manner of expression or design |
| **Inner Feelings** | how someone feels inside |
| **Temperament** | a person's or animal's natural disposition |
| **Use or Purpose** | why something is needed |
| **Parts** | components of an object |

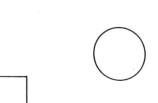

# Color

red
scarlet
cardinal
rosy
ruby
flushed
inflamed
carmine
cherry
coral
maroon
crimson

blue
royal blue
sky blue
powder blue
navy blue
robin's egg blue
turquoise
indigo blue
sapphire

yellow
golden
lemon yellow
jaundiced
tawny
cream-colored
buff
amber
canary yellow

green
emerald green
kelly green
chartreuse
lime green

purple
violet
plum
fuchsia
lavender
lilac
magenta
mauve
amethyst

orange
apricot
peach
flaming
copper
rust
tangerine

brown
mahogany
chocolate brown
tan
bronze
copper
chestnut brown
walnut
beige
coffee brown
hazel
taupe

black
ebony
sable
slate

gray
silver
ashen
dapple-gray

white
snow white
frosted
silvery
milky
alabaster
ivory
pearly
cream-colored
off-white

*Defining and Describing* ©Circuit Publications

Think about the words associated with **color**.
List some things that are:

red                    blue                    yellow                   green

_____   _____   _____   _____

_____   _____   _____   _____

_____   _____   _____   _____

_____   _____   _____   _____


orange                 gray                    black                    white

_____   _____   _____   _____

_____   _____   _____   _____

_____   _____   _____   _____

_____   _____   _____   _____


Use your imagination.  What color or colors come to mind
when you think of each of the following.  Why?

| sunshine | clouds | autumn | being sad |
| fire | spring | winter | the jungle |
| lipstick | summer | a pet | a king's palace |
| the ocean | the desert | a storm | a birthday party |


Sometimes colors are not clearly stated.  You have to imagine what color is actually
being identified.  Here are the names of some lipstick and nail polish colors.  What
color do you think they really are.  Why?

| Cherries jubilee | Juicy melon | Daydream pink | Maple magic |
| Country apple | Moonlit berry | Luscious peach | Ginger pink |

# Brightness

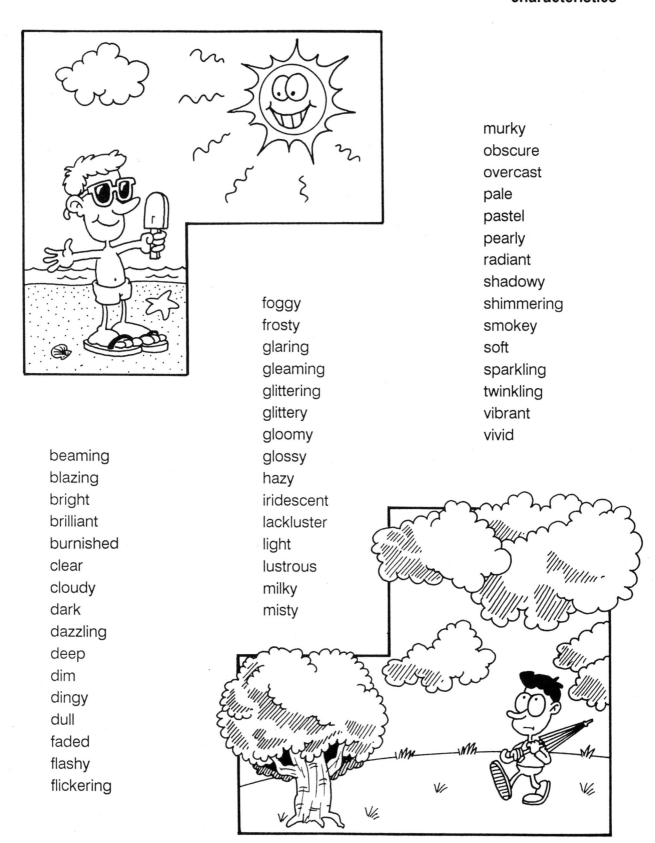

murky
obscure
overcast
pale
pastel
pearly
radiant
shadowy
shimmering
smokey
soft
sparkling
twinkling
vibrant
vivid

foggy
frosty
glaring
gleaming
glittering
glittery
gloomy
glossy
hazy
iridescent
lackluster
light
lustrous
milky
misty

beaming
blazing
bright
brilliant
burnished
clear
cloudy
dark
dazzling
deep
dim
dingy
dull
faded
flashy
flickering

*Defining and Describing*    © Circuit Publications

Think about the words that are associated with **brightness**.
Write some words that remind you of:

a beautiful, sunny summer day _____

a dismal, dreary rainy day _____

a brand new car _____

a diamond bracelet _____


Think of some words associated with *color* and with *brightness*.  Using some of these words, describe these objects

a cucumber's outside _____

a cucumber's inside _____

a watermelon's outside _____

a watermelon's inside _____

a hamburger before it's cooked _____

a hamburger after it's cooked _____

a parrot _____

a walnut _____

an evergreen tree _____

a hermit crab _____

apple blossoms _____

lemonade _____

a maple tree in the **spring** _____

a maple tree in the **autumn** _____

the sky on a clear day _____

the sky before a storm _____

a grasshopper _____

dandelions _____

a forest fire, out of control _____

# Size

petite
plump
portly
puny
reduced
roomy
scant
short
shrunken
skimpy
small
spacious
stout
stretched
stupendous
summarized
svelte
swollen
teeny
thick
thin
tiny
towering
vast
wee
wide

abbreviated
abundant
ample
big
bountiful
colossal
compact
condensed
cramped
dwarfed
enormous
expanded
gigantic
great

huge
humongous
large
little
long
mammoth
massive
measly
microscopic
mighty
miniature
monstrous
narrow
paltry

*Defining and Describing* © Circuit Publications

Think about words associated with **size**.  How could these words be used here?

One day a tiny mouse was running along a path in the woods.  Suddenly, the mouse looked up and saw, standing in the path, an elephant!  The mouse turned around and ran back home and told his friends about the elephant.

This elephant had noticed the little mouse.  He watched the mouse run back down the path and out of sight.  He was glad the mouse could turn and move so quickly.  He knew that if he would have stepped on this tiny creature his hoof would have indeed crushed it.

What are some words that might have gone through the elephant's mind as he thought of the size of the mouse?

_____
_____
_____
_____
_____
_____
_____
_____
_____

What are some of the words that the mouse might have used to tell about the elephant?

_____
_____
_____
_____
_____
_____
_____
_____
_____

# Shape

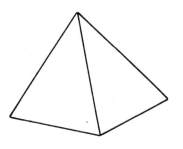

elliptical
erect
flat
forked
geodesic
heart-shaped
hexagon-shaped
hollow
level
molded
oblong
obtuse
octagon-shape
oval
pentagon-shaped

angular
arched
bell-shaped
bent
circular
coiled
cone-shaped
crooked
cubical
curved
cylindrical
diamond-shaped
dome-shaped
egg-shaped

pointed
pyramidal
rambling
rectangular
round
scalloped
solid
spherical
spiral
square
straight
symmetrical
triangular
tunnel-shaped
upright

*Defining and Describing*

Some things that we see every day or that we read about remind us of different shapes.  Think of the **shape** that each of these things has or is like.

a tire_____        a globe_____

a cereal box_____        an orange_____

a baseball field_____        ice cubes_____

a plate_____        a snake_____

a stop sign_____        a paper clip_____

a pie_____        eye glasses_____

a tent_____        a doughnut_____

an igloo_____        a chimney_____

a book_____        an envelope_____

**a Frisbee™**_____        contact lenses_____

a door_____        a mountain_____

an enclosed sports stadium_____

Are these **hollow** or **solid**?

a tennis ball
a baseball
a bowling ball
a football
a beach ball

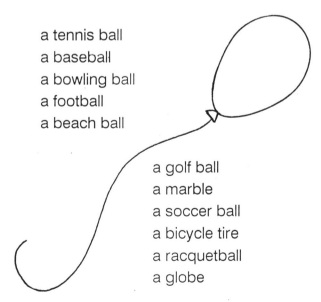

a golf ball
a marble
a soccer ball
a bicycle tire
a racquetball
a globe

a door knob
a sea shell
a tree trunk
a tunnel
a balloon
a pearl
a light bulb

**a Ping-Pong ball**
a baseball bat
an egg carton
a banana
a candy bar

# Texture or Touch

abrasive
absorbant
adhesive
bouffant
bristly
brittle
bumpy
chewy
coarse
congealed
creamy
crisp
crumbly
curdled
cushioned
delicate
effervescent
elastic

| | | |
|---|---|---|
| filmy | gummy | |
| fine | hard | scratchy |
| firm | juicy | shaggy |
| fizzy | lacquered | slippery |
| fleshy | limp | slushy |
| flexible | lumpy | smooth |
| floppy | matted | soupy |
| fluffy | moist | splintery |
| fluid | mushy | spongy |
| fragile | oily | springy |
| fuzzy | pliable | sticky |
| gelatinous | powdery | stringy |
| glassy | ridged | succulent |
| gooey | rocky | tender |
| grainy | rough | thick |
| granular | runny | tough |
| greasy | sandy | vaporous |
| gritty | scaled | velvety |

*Defining and Describing*

The **texture** or consistency of objects or substances can be determined by touch or feel. How does each of these things feel?

peanut butter_____     a beach_____

a brick_____     melting snow_____

a silk tie_____     crackers_____

pudding_____     a caterpillar_____

a pillow_____     a brush_____

cake mix_____     a computer floppy disc_____

glue_____     steam_____

Think about how some familiar things feel when you touch them.

clothes                                              furniture and appliances

<u>   *example:*  sweater</u>   <u>fuzzy_____</u>

_____  _____        _____  _____

_____  _____        _____  _____

_____  _____        _____  _____

_____  _____        _____  _____

_____  _____        _____  _____

food                                              plants and animals

_____  _____        _____  _____

_____  _____        _____  _____

_____  _____        _____  _____

_____  _____        _____  _____

_____  _____        _____  _____

# Weight

airy
buoyant
burdensome
cumbersome
featherweight
feathery
flimsy
heavy
hefty
lean
light
meager
mere
oppressive
ponderous
portable
scant
slight
slim
sparse
underweight
weightless
weighty
welterweight

*Defining and Describing* ©Circuit Publications

Think of the words that are associated with **weight**. Unscramble the words and complete the sentences below.

- The young boxer hopes to become _____ (egthirwweetl) champion of the world.

- The starving child weighed a _____ (reem) 30 pounds.

- How can that slight young girl lift that _____ (ythef) package?

- A _____ (vhyea) and _____ (bumroeemcs) trunk was left behind by the movers.

- Mike's beach ball didn't sink because it was _____ (ytboanu).

- The astronaut was _____ (lestwgeshi) during her space voyage.

- Our typewriter is _____ (blatpore) and easy to carry.

- That's quite a _____ (rosemudben) load. Are you sure you can carry it?

- Pauline was told to eat extra calories and drink milkshakes twice a day because she was _____ (rigunehdewt).

- Dante' could no longer carry his _____ (yehva) equipment after his back injury.

List some things that are:

| heavy | portable | light | |
|---|---|---|---|
| _____ | _____ | _____ | |
| _____ | _____ | _____ | buoyant *(floats on water)* |
| _____ | _____ | _____ | _____ |
| _____ | _____ | _____ | _____ |
| _____ | _____ | _____ | _____ |

# Material

agate
aluminum
angora
bamboo
bone
brass
brick
bronze
canvas
cardboard
chintz
clay
concrete
copper
corduroy
cork
cotton
crystal
denim
elastic
enamel
felt
gingham
glass

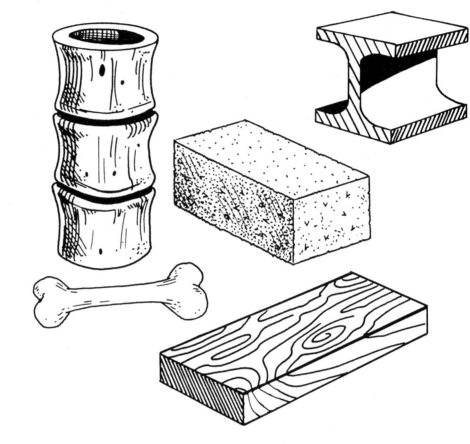

| gold | nylon | slate |
|------|-------|-------|
| gortex | paper | steel |
| hemp | pewter | stone |
| iron | plastic | straw |
| lace | platinum | suede |
| lead | plywood | taffeta |
| leather | polyester | tin |
| linen | porcelain | velvet |
| marble | rubber | vinyl |
| mineral | sand | wax |
| mohair | satin | wire |
| mud | silk | wood |
| nickle | silver | wool |

*Defining and Describing*

Think about different **materials** from which our things are made. Complete these exercises.

List some materials which might be needed to construct a home. Here are some things to think about.

| | |
|---|---|
| roof | bathtub |
| walls | light switches |
| floor | hinges |
| mirrors | switch plates |
| foundation | electrical system |
| patio doors | fireplace |
| wall coverings | floor coverings |

_____ _____ _____ _____

_____ _____ _____ _____

_____ _____ _____ _____

_____ _____ _____ _____

List some materials used in building automobiles. Here are some things to think about.

| | |
|---|---|
| engine | hubcaps |
| body | seats |
| windows | floor covering |
| tires | inside paneling |
| radio | steering wheel |

_____ _____ _____ _____

_____ _____ _____ _____

_____ _____ _____ _____

_____ _____ _____ _____

Think about the clothes you wear. Here are some materials from which clothes are made. What type of garments might be made from each of these materials. Think about why you would make certain garments from certain fabrics.

denim        silk        cotton        leather        lace

# Strength

dominating
durable
energetic
forceful
hardy
healthy
husky
immovable
indestructible
invigorated
invincible
inviolate
irrevocable
lasting
mighty
muscular
potent
powerful
resilient
resistant
robust
rugged
secure
solid
strong
stubborn
tenacious
tough
unbreakable
unconquerable
unyielding
vigorous
virile

ailing
breakable
faint
feeble
flabby
flaccid
fragile
frail
insecure
lame
lax
limp
passive
powerless
precarious
sickly
sluggish
soft
squeamish
unhealthy
unprotected
unsound
unstable
vulnerable
weak
wobbly
yielding

| T | H | P | O | W | E | R | F | U | L | I | S | E | C | U | R | E |
|---|---|---|---|---|---|---|---|---|---|---|---|---|---|---|---|---|
| T | N | G | O | W | R | H | S | Z | R | L | B | P | Q | O | D | R |
| W | P | V | I | G | O | R | O | U | S | G | R | C | N | S | O | E |
| T | H | Q | O | F | H | E | D | O | T | F | E | U | K | E | Q | B |
| M | O | M | U | S | C | U | L | A | R | W | A | B | H | N | R | M |
| L | S | O | R | N | F | G | I | E | O | R | K | L | T | E | Q | I |
| B | O | R | A | N | D | O | E | D | N | T | A | K | Y | R | B | G |
| W | R | J | O | W | S | T | O | U | G | H | B | I | X | G | R | H |
| F | O | R | C | E | F | U | L | C | N | S | L | S | O | E | R | T |
| Q | B | Z | O | F | E | D | N | G | L | H | E | A | L | T | H | Y |
| P | U | V | N | S | O | R | N | E | S | A | S | N | O | I | N | E |
| N | S | S | N | R | E | O | S | Q | Z | R | B | O | R | C | C | O |
| N | T | S | N | O | R | S | N | P | W | D | N | O | E | N | S | R |

Find the words associated with **strength** in the box at the left.

Find words in the box at the right that mean quite the **opposite** of **strong**.

| S | I | C | K | L | Y | S | H | E | N | S | O | V | Q | O |
|---|---|---|---|---|---|---|---|---|---|---|---|---|---|---|
| D | R | N | O | A | W | B | R | E | A | K | A | B | L | E |
| S | N | R | O | X | S | N | O | E | R | A | Q | O | D | F |
| S | N | F | O | E | R | S | D | F | N | S | F | E | O | D |
| X | O | V | D | I | N | S | E | C | U | R | E | W | O | Q |
| A | S | F | N | E | O | R | S | D | N | E | E | S | O | R |
| A | N | F | E | O | R | M | S | V | N | Q | B | Q | O | R |
| V | P | T | S | O | F | T | S | C | L | R | L | M | N | O |
| N | O | R | S | W | R | F | N | E | O | W | E | A | K | U |
| Q | U | N | H | E | A | L | T | H | Y | S | N | E | O | F |
| S | N | T | R | O | I | C | O | W | R | N | S | O | R | Z |
| P | O | W | E | R | L | E | S | S | X | O | R | N | M | E |

Just for fun, draw a picture of the perfect, fearless leader. What are some words you would use to describe him or her?

# Taste

# Smell

appetizing
bitter
bland
burnt
buttery
chocolatey
creamy
delicate
delicious
fresh
gingery
hot
light
luscious
mellow
minty
natural
nutty
palatable
peppery
rich
rotten
salty
savory
sharp
smoked
snappy
sour
spicy
spoiled
stale
strong
sweet
tangy
tart
tasty
zesty

aromatic
balmy
fetid
foul
fragrant
fruity
mild
moldy
musty
noxious
odorless
odorous
perfumey
pleasant
polluted
potent
pungent
putrid
rancid
rank
repulsive
rotten
scented
soapy
spicy
stinky
strong
suffocating
sweet-smelling

Find a word which might help describe each of the foods listed below.
Solve the puzzle.

**ACROSS**

1. old crackers
2. medicine
4. Roqufort cheese
6. a just-picked peach
8. pretzels
9. candy cane
11. brownies
12. yogurt
13. cheddar cheese
14. green apple
15. mustard
16. unseasoned broth

**DOWN**

1. vinegar
2. holiday cookies
3. taco sauce
5. gingerbread
7. Texas chili
8. ham
10. strawberries
13. sugar

What are some of your favorite foods?  How do they **taste**?

Think about words that remind us of various **smells.**
Unscramble the words and fill in the blank.

- Sue likes to smell only the fragrance of her perfume so she uses _____ (tesnucden) hand cream.

- The _____ (yipsc) smell of the spagetti sauce made me hungry.

- The air near the crowded highway smells _____ (tlopleud).

- I love looking at the interesting old things in Grandma's attic.  I don't mind the dust or the _____ (yumst) smell.


What are some words which might describe the **smell** of each of these?

_____

_____

_____

_____

_____

_____

_____

_____

_____

_____

_____

_____

*Defining and Describing*

# Sound

audible
bass
boisterous
clamorous
echoing
euphonious
harmonious
high-pitched
hoarse
howling

low-pitched
mellow
melodic
muffled
musical
noisy
obstreperous
resonant
resounding
roaring
shrill
silent
squeaky
strident
ultra sonic
vociferous

# Distance

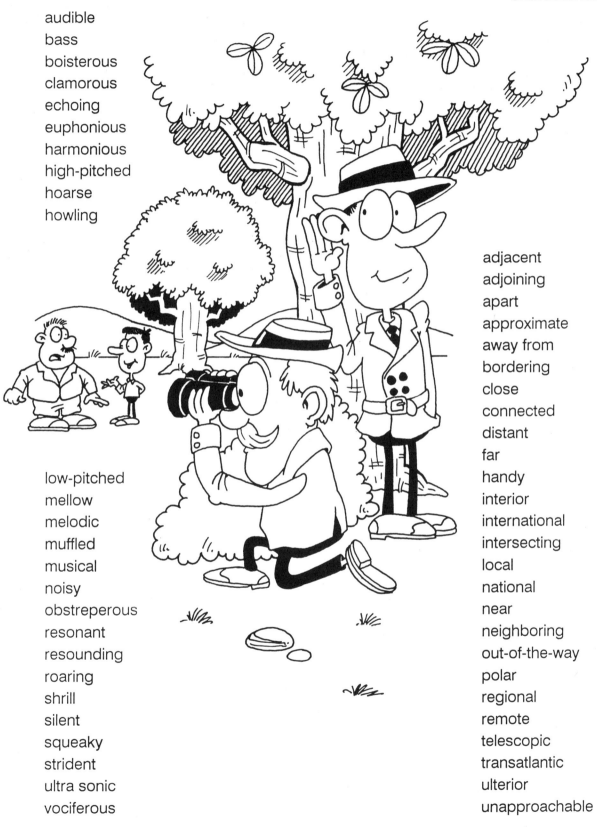

adjacent
adjoining
apart
approximate
away from
bordering
close
connected
distant
far
handy
interior
international
intersecting
local
national
near
neighboring
out-of-the-way
polar
regional
remote
telescopic
transatlantic
ulterior
unapproachable

Think about the words that describe different kinds of **sounds**. Select a word from the list which best completes each sentence.

■ I heard an _____ when I whistled in the canyon.

■ The inconsiderate people got involved in a _____ brawl disrupting our peaceful and _____ neighborhood.

■ I thought about the beautiful _____ sounds of Mozart's symphony for days after the concert.

■ A _____ little mouse lived in our basement for weeks.

■ The _____ motor boat stood out in the harbor where the sailboats sailed _____.

■ The cheerleader's voice was _____ after the game.

■ She played a cheerful _____ tune on the piano.

■ Turn the volume down. That music is much too _____!

■ She pulled her scarf over her face to keep warm. I couldn't understand everything she said because her voice was _____.

■ The wolves' _____ sounds could be heard for miles.

| | | | |
|---|---|---|---|
| echo | squeaky | melodic | quiet |
| clamorous | noisy | loud | muffled |
| hoarse | silently | howling | musical |

What are some pleasant, and some unpleasant sounds that you have heard? Why does each seem pleasant or unpleasant to you?

Think about the words associated with **distance**.

Look at the map of the Continental United States.
   Select a state and tell which states are nearest to this state.
   Which states are farthest from the state you selected?

Look at the map of Europe.
   Select a country and tell which countries are nearest to this country.
   Which European countries are farthest from the country you selected?

# Value

puny
rare
scarce
scrap
shabby
shoddy
showy
sought after
splendid
superb
superior
surplus
tacky
trivial
uncommon
unique
valuable
worthless

abundant
bargain
cheap
chintzy
choice
costly
dear
elegant
essential
expensive
exquisite
first-rate
gaudy
high quality
high-priced
in demand
in short supply
inexpensive

invaluable
junky
low priced
marked down
matchless
meager
measly
modest
one-of-a-kind
over-stocked
paltry
petty
plentiful
poor
precious
priceless
pricey
profitable

*Defining and Describing*          ©Circuit Publications

The **value** of objects or services is determined in different ways in different cultures. Generally, we determine value in two ways:

1. by the actual quality of an item and what materials and efforts went into its production,

2. by the concept of supply and demand. Items which are in demand and in short supply at a particular time will cost more than items which are plentiful but not in demand at the time.

Can you think of some words which might be associated with items in short supply?

_____

_____

_____

_____

Think of some words which might be associated with items in large supply.

_____

_____

_____

_____

Think of some words which might be associated with high quality.

_____

_____

_____

_____

List some words which tell of low quality.

_____

_____

_____

_____

Some of the most valuable things in our lives can not be given a particular dollar value. How would you describe the value of these special things?

health

friendship

freedom

clean air and water

our families

good neighbors

our wildlife

happy memories

# Position

middle
orbital
primary
prone
random
reclining
right
right-side-up
sagging
secondary
sedentary
separate
sequenced
solitary
stable
stooped over
submerged
sunken
supine
suspended
tilted
unbalanced
unstable
up-side-down
upright
vertical

clustered
detached
final
floating
hanging
high
horizontal
initial
lateral
leaning
left
level
longitudinal
low
medial

adjacent
attached
balanced
bordering
central

*Defining and Describing*

Think about words that are associated with an object's **position** in space. Find the words which will best describe these situations.

| X | U | O | R | B | I | T | A | L | O | N | R | O | S | G | Z |
|---|---|---|---|---|---|---|---|---|---|---|---|---|---|---|---|
| J | K | E | H | H | S | U | B | M | E | R | G | E | D | K | O |
| S | L | H | A | C | U | S | N | O | R | L | L | Q | E | D | U |
| D | U | Y | N | H | N | M | N | O | W | E | C | O | T | F | O |
| W | S | U | G | L | K | P | O | S | N | V | W | I | A | S | N |
| C | T | E | I | J | E | S | P | V | N | E | R | J | T | F | O |
| L | E | A | N | I | N | G | W | B | A | L | A | N | C | E | D |
| Y | R | B | G | F | N | M | I | D | D | L | E | L | H | P | Q |
| U | P | R | I | G | H | T | L | B | P | R | O | N | E | N | Y |
| D | R | E | C | L | I | N | I | N | G | B | O | V | D | P | W |

a bunch of grapes set on top of a bowl of fruit _____

a satellite which is circling the earth _____

a person lying on a beach, the sun shining on his face _____

a concrete foundation of a new house _____

a dog sitting between two boys _____

divers working to uncover the remains of a ship _____

a group of bats at rest _____

a garage, not connected to but 20 feet behind a house _____

the remarkable, very unusual tower in Pisa, Italy _____

**Dad** leaning back comfortably in his favorite chair _____

a soldier standing at attention _____

a submarine moving under the water's surface _____

a book sitting on a person's head _____

# Motion

agile
agitating
bumpy
cautious
churning
circular
constant
deliberate
dynamic
erratic
fast
firm
fixed
fluent
forward
graceful
gradual
immobile
intermittent
lateral
oscillating
permanent
perpetual
progressive
pulsating
quick
rapid

repetitive
reverse
revolving
rocking
settled
shaky
sideways
slow
sluggish
smooth
solid
spinning

stable
static
steadfast
steady
swaying
sweeping
swift
turbulent
twisting
variable
vibrating
wavy
well coordinated

*Defining and Describing*

Think of the words referring to **motion**. How would you best describe the type of motion in each of these? Select a word from the list below.

a waiter carrying a tray full of beverages _____

a tape recorder whose batteries were running out_____

a ferris wheel at a carnival _____

the Earth as it goes around the sun _____

a car driving along an unpaved road _____

a cradle _____

a gymnast _____

someone making his own butter _____

a race car _____

a plane traveling during a storm _____

a sky scraper during an earthquake _____

a car traveling in reverse _____

a large rock in the desert _____

someone walking up the street _____

a clothes dryer _____

a ballerina _____

water dripping from a faucet _____

river water _____

water boiling rapidly _____

an automatic washer _____

| agitating | coordinated | rapid | spinning |
| backward | fast | repetitive | steadfast |
| bumpy | flowing | rocking | steady |
| churning | forward | rotating | swaying |
| circular | graceful | sluggish | turbulent |

# Order

alphabetical
assorted
botched
businesslike
chaotic
classified
cluttered
complex
complicated
composed
confused
consecutive
converse
coordinated
decomposed
deranged
disorderly
hodgepodge
intricate

involved
irregular
jumbled
messy
methodical
muddled
normal
numerical
orderly
organized
perplexing
rank
regular
regulated
routine

sequenced
settled
simple
step by step
symmetrical
tangled
tumultuous
uniform
united
unsettled
untidy

*Defining and Describing* ©Circuit Publications

Think about the words associated with **order**. Complete these exercises.

Kate is usually a very organized person. However, last month she moved into an apartment. It seemed that everything about her and her surroundings was terribly disorganized. Her old apartment was damaged by a tornado and many items were scattered about and broken. She had very little time to find a new place to live, and moved into an apartment which had not been cleaned and prepared. Old furniture and belongings remained. A leaky pipe had damaged some of the ceiling, and it was beginning to crack and crumble. Kate's moving van was involved in an accident during the move and some of her things were damaged. Kate's new neighbor's friendly, but curious cat came into her apartment and knocked some things over as he investigated his new neighbor.

What are some words that might be used to talk about Kate's terrible time?

_____

_____

_____

_____

_____

Today, a month later, Kate is once again enjoying her well-organized life. Her lost or damaged items were replaced or repaired. The apartment has been cleaned, painted, the pipes and ceiling have been repaired. Kate's friends helped her to place everything as she wanted. She even bought some new accessories and decorations to make her apartment more attractive.

Now she is all ready for her friends to arrive at her first party. How would you describe Kate now?

_____

_____

_____

_____

_____

_____

Use your imagination and make up a story like this one. Use as many of these words as possible to talk about order and disorder.

Many things occur in a particular order. Think of some things that are generally arranged in alphabetical or numerical order.

Alphabetical (by letter)    Numerical (by number)

# Time

| | | |
|---|---|---|
| aboriginal | frequent | precocious |
| adult | fresh | prehistoric |
| aged | future | premature |
| ageless | hasty | present |
| alternate | historic | prevailing |
| ancestral | hourly | previous |
| ancient | immature | primeval |
| annually | immediate | primitive |
| Antebellum | imminent | prior |
| antique | impending | prompt |
| archaic | infantile | prospective |
| biennial | infrequent | punctual |
| brand-new | instant | recent |
| brief | juvenile | relic |
| bygone | late | remote |
| chronic | leisurely | rhythmic |
| classic | lifelong | seasonal |
| coexisting | mature | semi-annual |
| coincident | memorable | senile |
| commemorative | middle-aged | senior |
| concurrent | modern | serial |
| constant | momentary | short-lived |
| contemporary | monthly | sporadic |
| continuous | new | steady |
| current | newfangled | subsequent |
| cursory | next | sudden |
| cyclical | novel | synchronous |
| daily | obsolete | tardy |
| dated | old | temporary |
| declining | old-fashioned | time-honored |
| delayed | ongoing | traditional |
| early | original | transient |
| elderly | overdue | uninterrupted |
| eventual | part-time | up-to-date |
| expired | past | updated |
| extinct | periodic | veteran |
| fleeting | permanent | weekly |
| following | perpetual | young |
| former | preceding | youthful |

*Defining and Describing*

Think of the words associated with **time**. Complete these sentences.

young      instant      future      senior      commemorative

antique      daily      brief      current      historic

original      tardy      hasty      extinct      fresh

■ This _____ chair was built in the seventeenth century.

■ The beautiful painting is an _____ not a print or a copy.

■ On Wednesday _____ citizens get a 10% discount at the store.

■ The newspaper reports _____ events.

■ Steve had to stay after school because he was _____ three times last week.

■ Dinosaurs no longer live on our planet. They are _____ .

■ Maybe in the _____ we can travel to other planets.

■ We subscribe to a _____ newspaper.

■ The peaches were _____ and juicy. They were delicious!

■ Don't be _____ . Take your time so you won't make mistakes.

■ My mom and dad use _____ coffee because it is quick and easy to prepare.

■ I left a _____ message on the answering machine.

■ Many of our country's important documents were signed at this _____ building.

■ This is a _____ stamp honoring a famous composer.

■ David is 16 years old. He is too _____ to vote in the national election.

# Importance

central
chief
commanding
commonplace
earnest
essential
fair
foremost
frivolous
important
imposing
impressive
influential
insignificant
irrelevant
keynote
leading
main
major
meager
mediocre
nonessential
notable
ordinary
paramount
primary

principal
prominent
rare
salient
serious
significant
slight
solemn
substantial
trivial
unimportant
useful
useless
valuable

*Defining and Describing*

Think about the words which tell of **importance** or significance.  Select a word from the list which best completes each sentence.

ordinary      rare          prominent      mediocre       commanding
trivial        irrelevant    leading        keynote        insignificant

■ I don't know why they made such a fuss about my outfit.  I think it's just
_____.  I dress like this all the time.

■ What bothers me about Ted is that he always seems to talk about the
_____ items and neglects the important ones.

■ The archaeologists were pleased to discover a _____
fossil.  Only a few others of this species have ever been found.

■ Her comments had absolutely nothing to do with the subject of the discussion.
They were totally _____.

■ The _____ cause of traffic deaths in our state is
drunk driving.

■ Mrs. Daves is a very _____ citizen in our
community.  She was our mayor for six years and is now running for congress.

■ We were disappointed in the new musical.  We had hoped it would be a smash
hit, but it turned out to be only _____.

■ Your paragraph should contain the important information only.  Don't waste
time on _____ items.

■ Sarah is the _____ officer of her platoon.

■ We're so proud of our dad!  He was just asked to be the
_____ speaker at the fire fighters' convention next month.

Look at this year's calendar.  Identify the important dates.  Why is each one important?

# Appearance

absurd
appalling
aristocratic
attractive
awesome
awkward
becoming
bizarre
blase'
blemished
bored
charismatic
charming
clumsy
conspicuous
dainty
dazzling
deformed
delicate
demure
deplorable
dignified
disgusting
distinguished
dowdy
elegant
enhancing
evil
exquisite
feminine
funny
garish
gaudy
ghastly
gorgeous
graceful

grim
gross
grotesque
gruesome
haggard
hideous
homely
incredible
macho
magnificent
monstrous
mysterious
natural
nauseating
neat
obnoxious
obscene
offensive
pathetic
picturesque
poised
pretentious
quaint
repulsive
ridiculous
rowdy
scholarly
shocking
sloppy
slovenly
sneaky
soothing
splendid
strange
stuck up
sublime

tarnished
terrible
tidy
ugly
uninviting
unwieldy
virile
vulgar

*Defining and Describing*

Think about the words related to the **appearance** of something or someone.
Solve the puzzle.

| D | I | G | N | I | F | I | E | D | R | I | L | C | T | Z | P | M | D |
|---|---|---|---|---|---|---|---|---|---|---|---|---|---|---|---|---|---|
| I | T | H | W | O | F | M | C | N | E | O | S | H | R | O | F | N | A |
| S | V | M | D | N | E | P | S | N | F | I | D | A | I | N | T | Y | Z |
| T | U | G | R | A | C | I | O | U | S | Q | O | R | T | O | S | N | Z |
| I | S | M | C | N | S | O | S | U | B | L | I | M | E | S | O | R | L |
| N | T | O | A | N | M | X | W | X | A | C | O | I | R | N | S | O | I |
| G | O | R | G | E | O | U | S | S | P | L | E | N | D | I | D | R | N |
| W | S | N | E | P | S | O | O | T | H | I | N | G | S | M | O | W | G |
| I | M | N | P | W | S | N | S | O | E | V | X | S | R | L | D | N | E |
| S | S | M | E | P | D | E | M | U | R | E | G | N | E | N | E | A | T |
| H | B | P | I | C | T | U | R | E | S | Q | U | E | E | H | L | S | I |
| E | M | E | O | A | N | S | R | N | E | X | Q | U | I | S | I | T | E |
| D | A | B | X | E | S | C | H | S | Y | R | S | P | D | F | C | C | I |
| R | N | G | O | G | S | N | D | I | R | X | E | L | E | G | A | N | T |

| D | N | G | O | E | R | N | G | R | O | T | E | S | Q | U | E | R | W |
|---|---|---|---|---|---|---|---|---|---|---|---|---|---|---|---|---|---|
| S | N | R | S | N | G | E | R | F | T | E | F | E | N | L | V | E | D |
| W | O | B | N | O | X | I | O | U | S | S | M | R | E | O | I | D | E |
| S | P | R | M | D | U | G | S | H | O | E | N | S | D | L | L | I | J |
| P | E | R | E | P | U | L | S | I | V | E | S | R | E | M | P | C | E |
| A | F | N | E | O | S | F | E | G | R | U | E | S | O | M | E | U | K |
| T | M | P | M | E | S | O | G | M | E | T | S | P | A | W | S | L | P |
| H | O | R | R | I | B | L | E | M | N | S | O | E | N | H | L | O | E |
| E | S | M | E | N | O | S | N | E | R | O | H | I | D | E | O | U | S |
| T | E | R | R | I | B | L | E | F | N | E | O | S | E | Z | P | S | Q |
| I | M | O | N | E | O | S | N | G | U | G | L | Y | P | N | P | N | O |
| C | S | N | R | E | O | N | F | E | B | Q | G | A | W | D | Y | N | O |
| Q | B | L | E | M | I | S | H | E | D | Z | O | N | F | L | K | R | D |

# Style

artificial
artistic
casual
classic
commemorative
conservative
contemporary
conventional
crude
cultured
daring
dramatic
elaborate
elegant
fancy
fashionable
festive
formal
functional
gaudy
graceful
informal
modern
modest
natural

original
ornamental
plain
preppy
radical
refined
rugged
showy
simple
solemn
sophisticated
sporty

staid
stately
stilted
tacky
tailored
tasteful
traditional
trendy
typical
unique
unnatural
whimsical

*Defining and Describing*

Think about the words associated with **style**.  What are some words which would describe:

a charming old royal palace

_____

_____

_____

_____

_____

a small house in the city

_____

_____

_____

_____

_____

Sue's wild new outfit

_____

_____

_____

_____

my everyday clothes

_____

_____

_____

_____

Unscramble these opposites

traditional / *nerdom*_____

refined / *edruc*_____

ornamental / *talufnicno*_____

artificial / *luranta*_____

trendy / *cslicas*_____

whimsical / *molsen*_____

elegant / *yacty*_____

fancy / *ailpn*_____

conservative / *cirdala*_____

typical / *euuqin*_____

formal / *slacua*_____

elaborate / *lispem*_____

# Inner Feelings

afraid
amused
angry
ashamed
bored
comfortable
confident
confused
curious
disappointed
embarrassed
exasperated
frustrated
guilty
happy
hurt
interested
jealous
lonely
relieved
sad
satisfied
terrified
timid
undecided
upset
worried

*Defining and Describing*

Think about the words that express how we **feel** inside.  Read the sentences below and write a word telling how each one must feel.

Mrs. Lorez just won the lottery.

_____

Jim's pet parakeet flew away yesterday.

_____

Mother just caught Sparky, the family dog, chewing on her new shoes.

_____

Sally wonders what's in the odd-shaped package in the hall.

_____

The people watched the ugly dark smoke rise up into the clear blue sky.  They remember all the trash that they sent to the dump to be burned.

_____

Bill can't figure out how to work the math problems in his homework assignment.  He probably did not understand the lesson in class this morning.

_____

Pedro's TV is broken, his friends are all away on vacation, he's already read all his library books, and it's raining outside.

_____

Heather was home alone at night.  She heard a strange noise and thought it might be a burglar.

_____

Keesha is not sure what to get her mom for Mothers' Day, earrings, a scarf or perfume.

_____

The Jacksons had planned a picnic for today but it rained, so they cancelled their plans.

_____

| Now, see if you can think of some situations where someone might feel: | | | | |
|---|---|---|---|---|
| lonely | sad | happy | excited | comfortable |
| amused | afraid | upset | timid or shy | embarrassed |

# Temperament

aggressive
apathetic
callous
cheerful
cold
confident
considerate
cordial
creative
cruel
cynical
easy-going
enthusiastic
excitable
gentle
gloomy
grumpy
hardened

heartless
humble
ill-tempered
impatient
indifferent
intense
jolly
jovial
kind
laid back
lazy
lively
meek
melancholy
mellow
nervous
nonchalant
optimistic
passionate

patient
pompous
prudish
relaxed
romantic
sarcastic
sensitive
sentimental
serious
skeptical
smug
spirited
stoic
tolerant
trusting
uptight
vain
violent
warm

*Defining and Describing*

Think about the words that describe someone's **temperament**. Use these words to answer these questions.

Maggie makes people around her feel comfortable and happy. What are some characteristics which describe her temperament?

_____

_____

_____

_____

_____

The wicked witch threatened to turn the beautiful princess into a porcupine. What are some words which describe the queen's temperament?

_____

_____

_____

_____

_____

Sometimes when Jeff feels lonely he wishes some new people would move into his neighborhood. He wishes there would be a boy his age who would become his new friend. What does Jeff imagine that his friend would be like?

_____

_____

_____

_____

_____

# Use or Purpose

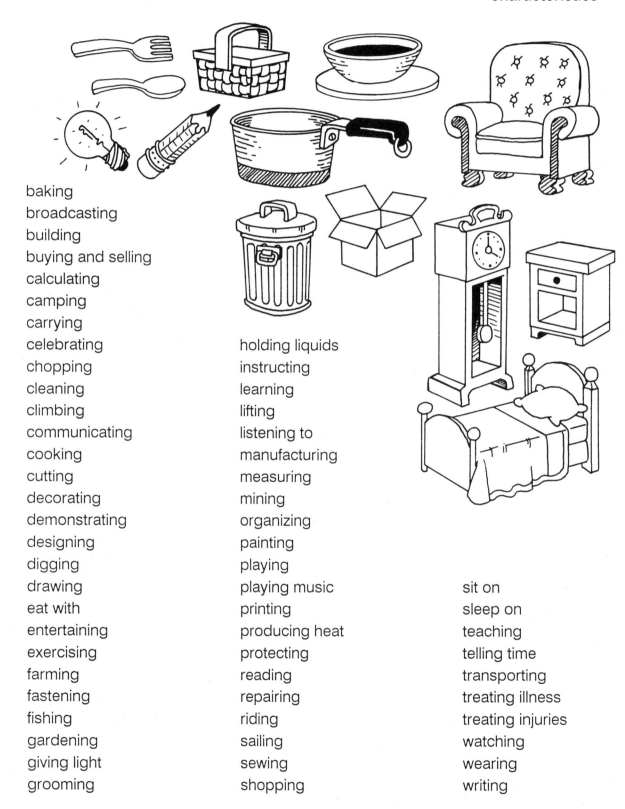

baking
broadcasting
building
buying and selling
calculating
camping
carrying
celebrating
chopping
cleaning
climbing
communicating
cooking
cutting
decorating
demonstrating
designing
digging
drawing
eat with
entertaining
exercising
farming
fastening
fishing
gardening
giving light
grooming

holding liquids
instructing
learning
lifting
listening to
manufacturing
measuring
mining
organizing
painting
playing
playing music
printing
producing heat
protecting
reading
repairing
riding
sailing
sewing
shopping

sit on
sleep on
teaching
telling time
transporting
treating illness
treating injuries
watching
wearing
writing

*Defining and Describing*

Think about words telling us how various things are **used**.
Complete the puzzle.

ACROSS
2.  A baby carriage
5.  A comb
6.  A burglar alarm
9.  An oven
10. A chalk board
11. Shelves
13. A shovel
14. A telephone
16. A math workbook
18. Balloons
20. Lumber
21. A hat
22. A pen
26. Drafting table
29. An apple
30. A furnace
31. A ladder
33. A wrench
34. A needle and thread

DOWN
1.  Printing press
2.  A tent
3.  A costume
4.  A recipe
7.  A bicycle
8.  A piano
9.  A radio
12. Music
15. A ruler
17. A pencil
19. A vacuum cleaner
21. A television
23. Weights
24. A truck
25. A plow
27. A rake
28. Ornaments
32. Money

# Parts

| | | |
|---|---|---|
| antennae | banister | battery |
| antlers | ceiling | brakes |
| arms | chimney | carburetor |
| bones | doors | fenders |
| ears | drawer | filter |
| eyes | floor | gear |
| feet | hinge | handle bars |
| fins | knob | hood |
| hands | latch | motor |
| head | rack | pedals |
| heart | railing | radiator |
| hoofs | roof | seat |
| horns | socket | spark plug |
| legs | stairs | steering wheel |
| lungs | switch | tank |
| muscles | thermostat | trunk |
| neck | walls | wheels |
| nose | windows | |
| paws | wires | buckle |
| ribs | | buttons |
| shoulders | blade | collar |
| skin | clasp | cuffs |
| stomach | clip | heel |
| tail | dial | pockets |
| teeth | handle | sleeves |
| tentacle | lever | snap |
| | prong | sole |
| | spout | zipper |
| | branch | |
| | leaf | |
| | petals | |
| | root | |
| | seed | |
| | stem | |
| | trunk | |

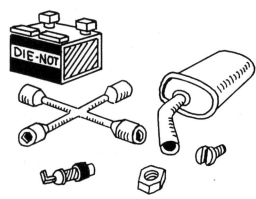

*Defining and Describing*    © Circuit Publications

Think about the words which identify **parts** of an animal, a house, a plant, or a garment. Unscramble the words.

dhea_____

lait_____

swap_____

srea_____

heett_____

thear_____

noseb_____

thoum_____

tchoams_____

lalw_____

downwi_____

glicne_____

olrfo_____

foro_____

sistar_____

yichenm_____

glinair_____

charbn_____

mest_____

tealp_____

nurtk_____

flea_____

edes_____

dhoo_____

ketopc_____

locral_____

tobutn_____

prizep_____

clubek_____

THERE SURE ARE A LOT OF WORDS TO HELP TELL EACH OTHER ABOUT THINGS, AREN'T THERE? I HOPE I CAN RE-MEMBER HOW TO DEFINE SOMETHING...

...I THINK THIS IS RIGHT

- First, I say the word (the subject of the definition) that I'm defining.
- Next, I tell my listener the category into which the word fits.
- Finally, I list the characteristics which make my subject special.

AN APPLE IS A FRUIT WHICH IS ROUND, RED ON THE OUTSIDE, WHITE ON THE INSIDE, HAS SKIN, SEEDS AND A STEM, IS GOOD TO EAT AND TO USE FOR BAKING PIES.

A RABBIT IS A SMALL ANIMAL WHICH HAS SOFT FUR, LONG EARS, AND A STUBBY TAIL.

OKAY SO FAR?

GREAT !

*Defining and Describing*

YOU'RE ALL SET! I'M SURE YOU CAN DEFINE JUST ABOUT ANYTHING THAT YOU'VE LEARNED ABOUT HERE ON EARTH, BUT, HERE ARE A FEW HINTS TO MAKE DEFINING A LITTLE EASIER...

Sometimes you might need to define something sort of complicated that has two or more important parts. So, when this happens, go ahead and say the name of the subject, the category and give the characteristics of the parts one by one, telling the listener how the parts are related. Like this...

"A bicycle is a vehicle with a tubular metal frame which is connected to (or mounted on) two narrow wheels, one behind the other. It also has a seat, handle bars and pedals."

And one more important thing. When you try to define things and you're not exactly sure of what classification or category they belong to, it's okay with kids when you say that things are **things** and that stuff is **stuff**. But grown-ups, especially important grown-ups like teachers don't like to hear you say **thing** and **stuff**. They like you to say more sophisticated words. Here are some ways of saying **thing** and **stuff**:

Words you can use instead of **thing**

| | | |
|---|---|---|
| object | concept | implement |
| notion | instrument | item |
| structure | entity | creature |
| circumstance | situation | body |
| issue | element | incident |
| device | being | unit |
| event | gadget | |

Words you can use instead of **stuff**

| | | |
|---|---|---|
| substance | mass | material |
| mixture | combination | solution |
| gas | paraphernalia | apparatus |
| gear | matter | liquid |
| goods | | |

Look at this list of words. These words should give you ideas of how to refer to something when you're not sure of its classification.

| | | | | |
|---|---|---|---|---|
| object | notion | structure | circumstance | issue |
| device | event | concept | instrument | entity |
| situation | element | being | gadget | implement |
| item | creature | body | incident | unit |
| substance | mixture | gas | gear | goods |
| mass | combination | paraphernalia | matter | material |
| solution | apparatus | liquid | | |

On the line beside each of these words write a word from the list above which might be used to refer to the word.

car_____          sand_____

salad dressing_____          bumble bee_____

copper_____          pencil_____

jelly_____          calculator_____

salamander_____          shampoo_____

smog_____          fishing tackle_____

wedding_____          wax_____

accident_____          coin_____

door knob_____          camera_____

grease_____          shirt_____

medicine_____          coal_____

water vapor_____          ink_____

paste_____          spoon_____

*Defining and Describing*

See if you can guess what's being defined here.  Fill in the blank.

- A _____ is a tool for pounding consisting of a metal head and a handle.

- A _____ is a piece of furniture with a back and a seat intended for one person to sit on.

- _____ is a soft sweet food made with flour, eggs, milk, and flavoring or fruit.

- A _____ is a building made of brick, wood or other building materials used as a shelter for motor vehicles.

- A _____ is a rugged motor vehicle for transporting loads of materials.

- _____ is an outdoor sport played with a small hard ball and a set of clubs.

- A _____ is a musical instrument made of brass consisting of a looped tube which ends in a flare.

- A _____ is a musical instrument made of wood which has string made of nylon or metal plucked with fingers.

- _____ is a style of music which is syncopated and very rhythmic.

- A _____ is a kitchen utensil with a broad, flexible blade for spreading or blending foods.

- _____ is a fuel which is a thin oil made from petroleum.

- A _____ is a fastener which is a small disk or knob.

| | | | |
|---|---|---|---|
| pudding | guitar | button | spatula |
| hammer | trumpet | chair | kerosene |
| garage | truck | golf | jazz |

See if you can guess what's being defined here.
Fill in the subject and the classification.

■ A _____ is a _____ that is large, round, sour, has yellow rind, juicy pulp, white seeds.

■ A _____ is a _____ that is small, red, fleshy, sweet, somewhat pyramid shaped with straw-like particles on the skin.

■ A _____ is a _____ that is used to sit on, usually made of wood, has a back, a seat and four legs.

■ A _____ is a _____ that tells time, has a face with numbers and hands which are connected to a device which runs by battery or electric power.

■ A _____ is a _____ that carries passengers or cargo, travels by air, has wings, an engine or engines, landing gear, and is made of metal.

■ A _____ is a _____ that is used for carrying objects or materials, made of wood, cane or straw woven together, and often has a handle.

■ A _____ is a _____ that is used for holding flowers, made of glass, clay, or plastic, is tall with an opening at the top.

■ A _____ is a _____ that joins two sides of a garment, has a sliding part in the center, is made of metal or plastic tabs (sometimes called teeth) which interlock.

■ _____ is a _____ that is a soapy liquid, often has a perfumey scent and is used for washing one's hair.

■ An _____ is a _____ having a flat bottom which is heated and used for pressing cloth.

**name**

| grapefruit | strawberry | chair | airplane | basket |
| vase | zipper | shampoo | iron | cloth |

**classification**

| substance | fastener | furniture | fruit | vehicle |
| device | container | appliance | | |

*Defining and Describing*

Complete these definitions. Fill in the characteristics.

■ A cat is a small furry animal that has a long tail,_____
ears, whiskers, moves gracefully, purrs when contented and is a nice pet.

■ An elephant is a large animal with tusks, a trunk, large ears, rough
_____ skin.

■ A peach is a small _____ fruit with a large seed in the
center and fuzzy skin.

■ A rake is a tool used for gathering leaves or hay having teeth at one end and a
_____ handle.

■ A banana is a fruit which is yellow, has a _____ texture and thick skin.

■ A caramel is a food which tastes sweet, is cube-shaped and has a
_____ texture.

■ A knife is a utensil with a _____ metal blade at one end
and has a short handle.

■ A brick is a small, red, rectangle-shaped building material made of
_____.

■ A belt is something to wear around one's waist. It is
_____, made of leather, and has a buckle.

■ A bus is a large oblong motor vehicle for _____ many
passengers.

■ Paper is a _____, flexible material used for writing or
packaging which comes in sheets and is made from wood pulp.

■ A pencil is something to write with. It is small, _____,
made of wood and is light weight.

**characteristics**

| rod-shaped | sharp | pointed | sweet-tasting |
| soft | narrow | thin | transporting |
| clay | chewy | long | gray |

Complete these definitions. Find the name of what's being defined, the category or characteristic and fill in the blanks.

- A horse is a large _____ which can be ridden. It has short hair, large eyes an oblong-shaped head and can _____.

- An _____ is a dome-shaped structure made of _____ in which Eskimo families live.

- A pie is a food made of _____ and _____ which is round, tastes sweet, is cut in slices and eaten for dessert.

- A lime is a small green _____ which tastes _____.

- A _____ is something to read. It is small, rectangle-shaped, has a hard cover and many printed _____.

- A _____ is something to give light. It is long, cylinder-shaped, made of _____ and has a wick down the center.

- A dog is a _____ animal often kept as a pet. It can be large or small, have long or short hair and is usually _____ by nature.

- Flour is a powdery white substance made from _____ and used for _____.

- Vinegar is a sour _____ used for _____ dressings.

- _____ is a creamy yellow food with a _____ taste which is spread on sandwiches.


| | | | | |
|---|---|---|---|---|
| liquid | gallop | book | candle | baking |
| igloo | pages | mustard | salad | ice |
| spicy | filling | animal | grain | canine |
| friendly | fruit | wax | crust | sour |

*Defining and Describing*

Find some words and ideas in the list that will help you define the objects pictured below. Use words more than once if necessary.

| | | | |
|---|---|---|---|
| animal | food | hoofed | made from wood |
| utensil | strong | greasy | cracks nut shells |
| has a mane | white | two handles | can be ridden |
| sweet | granular | creamy | cylinder-shaped |
| metal | dairy product | squeeze it | rectangle-shaped sticks |
| long handle | sweetens | metal | for gathering leaves |
| teeth (prongs) | garden tool | yellow | rolls out dough |

sugar

_____
_____
_____
_____
_____

rolling pin

_____
_____
_____
_____

rake

_____
_____
_____
_____

horse

_____
_____
_____
_____

nut cracker

_____
_____
_____

butter

_____
_____
_____
_____

Find some words and ideas in the list that will
help you define the objects pictured below.

utensil            graceful        sleeves         used for toasting bread
thick metal blade  tool            holds liquids   used for serving soup
made of cotton     large beak      electric cord   metal or plastic bowl
clothing           appliance       animal(bird)    used for chopping
spout              container

**blouse**

_____

_____

_____

**swan**

_____

_____

_____

**toaster**

_____

_____

_____

**ax**

_____

_____

_____

**pitcher**

_____

_____

_____

**ladle**

_____

_____

_____

*Defining and Describing*

Help this chef define these foods:

An orange is a fruit that_____

_____

_____

Lettuce is a vegetable that_____

_____

_____

A hamburger is a meat that_____

_____

_____

Bread is a food that_____

_____

_____

Corn flakes is a food that_____

_____

_____

Pie is a dessert that_____

_____

_____

Help this carpenter define these tools:

A saw is a tool that_____

_____

_____

A hammer is a tool that_____

_____

_____

A screw driver is a tool that_____

_____

_____

A drill is a tool that_____

_____

_____

A chisel is a tool that_____

_____

_____

A level is a tool that_____

_____

_____

*Defining and Describing*

Help this girl define things to wear:

A skirt is a garment that_____

_____

_____

A scarf is something to wear that_____

_____

_____

A coat is a garment that_____

_____

_____

A robe is something to wear that_____

_____

_____

A T shirt is a something to wear that_____

_____

_____

Mittens are things to wear_____

_____

_____

Help this scientist define
these substances:

Water is a substance that_____

_____

_____


Dynamite is a substance that_____

_____

_____


Chlorophyll is a substance that_____

_____

_____


Sand is a substance that_____

_____

_____


Pulp is a substance that_____

_____

_____

Help this naturalist define
these animals:

A zebra is an animal that_____

_____

_____


A crab is an animal that_____

_____

_____


A cat is an animal that_____

_____

_____


A turtle is an animal that_____

_____

_____


A kangaroo is an animal that_____

_____

_____


A giraffe is an animal that_____

_____

_____

Define some things in your home.

A cookie is_____

_____

_____

A can opener is _____

_____

_____

A pizza slicer is_____

_____

_____

A cup is_____

_____

_____

A table is_____

_____

_____

A rain coat is_____

_____

_____

NOW **I'LL** CHALLENGE **YOU**. GUESS WHAT I'M THINKING OF.
- A TOOL
- CYLINDER SHAPED
- HAS A PRONG IN THE CENTER
- HAS A CIRCLE OF PRONGS AT ONE END
- POWER TRANSFORMER
- MADE OF CINJULUM
- LIGHT WEIGHT
- USED FOR CHARGING ZOLOMETERS

I HAVE NO IDEA...
WHAT IS IT?

Have some
fun! Make
up
definitions
for some
objects or
creatures
that might
exist on
another
planet.
Use your
imagination
!

IT'S A JAXATROL !

WAIT...
WE DON'T HAVE JAXATROLS HERE ON EARTH. WE DON'T EVEN HAVE ZOLOMETERS !

Remember how to define...

| | | name of | |
| --- | --- | --- | --- |
| __name__ | is | __classification__ | __characteristics__ . |

YOU KNOW, I'M REALLY LEARNING A LOT ABOUT THINGS HERE ON EARTH. EVERYONE SEEMS TO BE WORKING HARD TO MAKE THIS A NICE PLACE TO LIVE. PEOPLE WORK TOGETHER. THEY TAKE CARE OF THE ANIMALS, THEY EVEN PLANT FLOWERS AND TREES AND TAKE CARE OF THEM.

EARTH PEOPLE ARE OKAY! I'M GOING TO HAVE SO MUCH TO TALK ABOUT WHEN I GET BACK TO SRAM.

'GLAD YOU LIKE US AND OUR PLANET. TELL ME ABOUT SOMETHING YOU LIKE ESPECIALLY WELL.

THAT'S HARD. THERE ARE SO MANY THINGS. BUT THERE IS ONE THING...

THERE IS THIS DOG THAT KEEPS FOLLOWING ME AROUND. AND, WHEN I STOP AND SIT DOWN THIS DOG JUST STOPS AND SITS NEXT TO ME, WAITS FOR ME TO GET UP, THEN HE GETS UP TOO AND COMES WITH ME UNTIL I LEAVE THE PARK. THEN HE STANDS THERE AND WATCHES ME WALK AWAY.

TELL ME ABOUT THAT DOG, MAZEY.

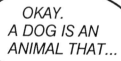

OKAY. A DOG IS AN ANIMAL THAT...

WAIT A MINUTE - YOU DON'T NEED TO **DEFINE** THE WORD DOG, I ALREADY KNOW WHAT A DOG IS, JUST **DESCRIBE** THIS SPECIAL DOG FOR ME SO I KNOW MORE ABOUT HIM.

WHAT DOES **DESCRIBE** MEAN? HOW SHOULD I DESCRIBE SOMETHING?

*Defining and Describing*

DESCRIBE MEANS TO TELL OR WRITE ABOUT SOMETHING. YOU DESCRIBE A PARTICULAR THING WHEN YOUR LISTENER ALREADY KNOWS WHAT IT IS YOU'RE TALKING ABOUT. I ALREADY KNOW WHAT DOGS ARE SO YOU DON'T HAVE TO **DEFINE** A DOG FOR ME. BUT I'M INTERESTED IN THE DOG THAT FOLLOWS YOU AROUND THE PARK. I'D LIKE TO KNOW WHAT HE LOOKS LIKE AND WHAT IS SPECIAL ABOUT THIS DOG. SO, WHEN YOU **DESCRIBE** A PARTICULAR OBJECT OR CREATURE, ALL YOU NEED TO DO IS TELL OR WRITE THE CHARACTERISTICS THAT MAKE THIS PARTICULAR CREATURE OR THING SPECIAL.

THAT'S EASY! OKAY, NOW I'LL TELL YOU ABOUT THIS DOG. HE'S BIG, ABOUT 2 FEET HIGH AND ABOUT 3 FEET LONG. HE HAS CURLY BLACK AND WHITE FUR, BROWN EYES, SOFT FLOPPY EARS, AND A LONG BUSHY TAIL THAT IS SORT OF CURVED UPWARD. HIS MOUTH IS CURVED UP ON THE SIDES SO IT LOOKS LIKE HE IS SMILING ALL THE TIME. AND, HE HAS A VERY GENTLE, FRIENDLY DISPOSITION. HOW'S THAT?

THAT WAS A FINE DESCRIPTION! I CAN CLOSE MY EYES AND PICTURE THAT DOG! GIVING A GOOD DESCRIPTION IS LIKE PAINTING A PICTURE IN YOUR LISTENER'S MIND. CAN YOU DESCRIBE ANYTHING ELSE THAT YOU SAW AT THE PARK?

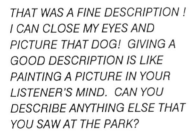

I CAN DESCRIBE THE BENCH WHERE I SIT AND LOOK AT THE DUCKS ON THE POND. IT'S A LONG NARROW BENCH. THE SEAT AND THE BACK ARE MADE OF WOODEN SLATS CONNECTED TO A METAL FRAME. THE LEGS ARE MADE OF METAL. THE WOOD IS PAINTED BRIGHT RED AND THE LEGS AND METAL FRAME ARE BLACK. THE BENCH ALSO HAS BLACK ARMRESTS, ONE ON EACH END.

...AND THIS BIG TREE.

THIS TREE IS ABOUT 20 FEET TALL, HAS A LARGE ROUND ROUGH TRUNK. AT THE TOP OF THE TRUNK ARE A FEW LARGE BRANCHES WHICH REACH OUT IN ALL DIRECTIONS. ON EACH LARGE BRANCH THERE ARE MANY, MANY SMALLER BRANCHES. EACH BRANCH HAS MANY LARGE, POINTED BRIGHT GREEN LEAVES ON IT. THIS TREE IS EVEN MORE SPECIAL BECAUSE THERE ARE FOUR BIRDS' NESTS THAT I CAN SEE WHEN I STAND NEXT TO THE TREE, ONE ON EACH LARGE BRANCH.

List some characteristics that will help you describe some familiar things in your neighborhood.

**stop sign**

color_____

size_____

shape_____

material_____

use or purpose_____

parts_____

**mail box**

color_____

shape_____

material_____

parts_____

use or purpose_____

size_____

**doughnuts**

shape_____

color_____

material_____

texture_____

taste_____

smell_____

**garden hose**

use or purpose_____

shape_____

size_____

color_____

material_____

parts_____

**a sidewalk**

position_____

use or purpose_____

size_____

shape_____

material_____

color_____

**a fence**

position_____

use or purpose_____

material_____

size_____

shape_____

color_____

Choose one of the items above and write a description.
Use the list of characteristics to help you write a description.

Pretend like you are telling a friend about some animals that you saw at the zoo. Think of some of the characteristics that would help you tell someone how each animal looked.

HINTS...
size
color
parts
motion
touch

**elephant**

_____

_____

_____

_____

**giant polar bear**

_____

_____

_____

_____

**monkey**

_____

_____

_____

_____

**snake**

_____

_____

_____

_____

Write a description of one of these animals.

_____

_____

_____

_____

_Defining and Describing_

Describe some things in your classroom.
Use this list for ideas.

| HINTS... | | | |
|---|---|---|---|
| color | weight | distance | importance |
| brightness | material | value | appearance |
| size | strength | position | style |
| shape | taste | motion | inner feelings |
| texture | smell | order | temperament |
| touch | sound | time | use or purpose |
| | | | parts |

■ Your desk at school

_____

_____

_____

■ One of your school books

_____

_____

_____

■ The clock in your classroom

_____

_____

_____

■ A bulletin board in your classroom

_____

_____

_____

■ The person who sits next to you in class

_____

_____

_____

Describe some things in your home.
Use this list for ideas.

HINTS...

| color | weight | distance | importance |
| brightness | material | value | appearance |
| size | strength | position | style |
| shape | taste | motion | inner feelings |
| texture | smell | order | temperament |
| touch | sound | time | use or purpose |
| | | | parts |

■ Your kitchen table

_____

_____

_____

■ Your front door

_____

_____

_____

■ A clock in your house

_____

_____

_____

■ Something in the living room

_____

_____

_____

■ Something in the kitchen

_____

_____

_____

*Defining and Describing*

NOW, I'LL DESCRIBE SOMETHING A LITTLE MORE COMPLICATED FOR YOU. SEE IF YOU CAN PICTURE THIS... MY DAD MADE ME A SPECIAL CABINET FOR MY ROOM. IT'S WHERE I KEEP ALL MY FAVORITE THINGS.

IT LOOKS LIKE THIS. IT'S ABOUT SIX FEET TALL AND ABOUT THREE FEET WIDE. IT'S MADE OF WOOD AND PAINTED RED. THE BOTTOM PART IS A CABINET WITH TWO DOORS. EACH DOOR HAS A SILVER KNOB. THE INSIDE OF THE CABINET IS PAINTED WHITE. WHEN YOU OPEN THE CABINET DOORS YOU SEE A SHELF WITH GAMES ON IT, AND A BOTTOM WITH BOXES WHERE I KEEP MY BASEBALL CARDS, MY POST CARD COLLECTION, MY KALEIDO-SCOPE, AND MY MICROSCOPE. ON THE INSIDE OF THE DOORS ARE SOME PICTURES FROM CAMP LAST SUMMER.

THE TOP PART OF THE CABINET HAS A BACK, SIDES AND THREE SHELVES. TWO OF THE SHELVES HAVE BOOKS ON THEM AND MY MODEL CAR COLLECTION IS ON THE TOP SHELF.

SOUNDS NICE. THAT WAS QUITE A DESCRIPTION ! IT MUST BE HARD TO DESCRIBE SOMETHING COMPLICATED LIKE THIS CABINET.

IT'S NOT A HARD AS IT SOUNDS. THERE'S A TRICK TO IT...

WELL, LET ME IN ON IT !

THAT SOUNDS A LOT LIKE HAVING TO **DEFINE** SOMETHING COMPLICATED.

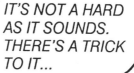

WHEN YOU WANT TO DESCRIBE SOMETHING COMPLICATED, SOMETHING WITH MORE THAN ONE MAIN PART, TELL YOUR LISTENER WHAT YOU'RE GOING TO DESCRIBE AND TRY TO GIVE ONE OR MORE CHARACTERISTICS THAT APPLY TO THE ENTIRE OBJECT, LIKE WHAT IT'S MADE OF, OR MAYBE WHAT COLOR. THEN DESCRIBE THE OBJECT, ONE PART AT A TIME. BE SURE TO TELL YOUR LISTENER HOW THE PARTS ARE RELATED TO EACH OTHER.

RIGHT !

Try to describe these complicated objects.

■ A freight train

*Remember, a freight train has many different types of cars, each for carrying different types of freight or cargo.*

_____

_____

_____

_____

_____

_____

_____

_____

_____

■ A personal computer

*Look at a computer in your classroom, the library, or the office. Be sure you know the name of each part or component.*

_____

_____

_____

_____

_____

_____

_____

_____

_____

Describe these complicated objects.

■ a sailboat

*Remember, the hull of the boat moves when the sails catch the wind.*

_____

_____

_____

_____

_____

_____

■ a helicopter

_____

_____

_____

_____

_____

_____

_____

■ a flag

_____

_____

_____

_____

_____

_____

Use your imagination.  Design and describe a costume you would wear to a wonderful, fantastic costume party.

*Defining and Describing*

SPEAKING OF DESCRIBING THINGS THAT ARE COMPLICATED, I'M SURE YOU'LL WANT TO DESCRIBE PLACES LIKE ROOMS, YARDS, OR BUILDINGS. THERE'S A TRICK TO THAT TOO...

FIRST, PRETEND THAT YOU'RE STANDING IN ONE PARTICULAR SPOT ON OR NEAR WHAT YOU'RE DESCRIBING - LIKE IN A DOORWAY, IN FRONT OF AND FACING A BUILDING, IN THE CENTER OR OFF TO THE SIDE OF AN OUTDOOR AREA, ETC.

THEN, DESCRIBE WHAT YOU'D SEE ON YOUR RIGHT, YOUR LEFT, IN FRONT OF YOU, ABOVE AND BELOW YOU, REMINDING YOUR LISTENER OF WHERE YOU'RE POSITIONED.

IF NECESSARY, CHANGE YOUR POINT OF VIEW DURING THE DESCRIPTION. THINGS LOOK DIFFERENT FROM DIFFERENT POINTS OF VIEW. PERHAPS YOU WISH TO DESCRIBE SOMETHING THAT COULD NOT BE SEEN FROM YOUR FIRST POINT OF VIEW LIKE THE UPPER FLOOR OF A BUILDING OR HOUSE. BE SURE TO TELL YOUR LISTENER THAT YOU'VE CHANGED YOUR POINT OF VIEW AND TELL HOW THIS POSITION IS RELATED TO YOUR FIRST POINT OF VIEW.

I'LL DESCRIBE MY 4TH GRADE CLASSROOM FOR YOU...

STANDING IN FRONT OF THE CLASSROOM BEHIND THE TEACHER'S DESK, I SEE YELLOW WALLS, A LIGHT WOOD FLOOR AND A WHITE CEILING. ON MY LEFT I SEE FOUR TALL NARROW WINDOWS. UNDER THE FIRST THREE WINDOWS IS A LONG TABLE FOR THE COMPUTER AND SOME SMALL SHELVES FOR COMPUTER MATERIALS. LOOKING STRAIGHT AHEAD, I SEE FIVE ROWS OF LIGHT TAN DESKS, FIVE DESKS IN EACH ROW. I ALSO SEE A LARGE BULLETIN BOARD ACROSS THE WHOLE BACK OF THE ROOM. OUR DRAWINGS AND PAINTINGS FROM ART CLASS ARE ON THE BULLETIN BOARD. ON MY RIGHT, I SEE TWO BROWN DOORS, ONE TOWARD THE FRONT AND ONE TOWARD THE BACK OF THE ROOM. BETWEEN THE DOORS, I SEE A GREEN CHALK BOARD. THE SAME GREEN CHALKBOARD IS ALL THE WAY ACROSS THE FRONT OF THE ROOM.

I SEE.

There are many different school
buildings and many different
classrooms. They are the same
in some ways but each is
different in special ways.

Describe your classroom.
Remember to tell where you are standing, your point of view.

_____

_____

_____

_____

_____

_____

_____

_____

Describe your school building.
Try describing the building from different points of view.

_____

_____

_____

_____

_____

_____

_____

_____

*Defining and Describing*

Describe your school gym and playground. Look at these places from different points of view. Try to create a *picture* of the school gym or playground from your point of view.

Describe the gym.

_____

_____

_____

_____

_____

_____

_____

_____

Describe the playground.

_____

_____

_____

_____

_____

_____

_____

_____

Think of places in or around your home.  Describe a room, the basement, your yard, or the outside of your house. Remember to state your point of view.

"I'm describing_____."

_____
_____
_____
_____
_____
_____
_____
_____
_____
_____

"I'm describing_____."

_____
_____
_____
_____
_____
_____
_____
_____
_____

*Defining and Describing*

Describe the grocery store where your
family shops, first from the outside,
then from the inside.

_____

_____

_____

_____

_____

_____

_____

_____

Pretend like you're a pilot.  Describe your town as you see it from the air.  Describe this
town as you see it from your car as you're driving.

_____

_____

_____

_____

_____

_____

_____

_____

_____

This is about how a place could seem different from different points of view.

Mr. Conway, the president of a small company is about six feet tall. It was important that his office was conveniently arranged. One Friday afternoon he looked around the office to make sure everything was in place. He walked over to the window and looked out. From where he stood he could look over shrubs outside and see the baseball diamond where the local high school team played and practiced. He watched for a minute then reached up to pull the cord which closed the drapes. He looked at the shelves next to the window and straightened his business record books. He glanced at his reference books which were used often. These were on the second shelf from the top.

He looked across the room and saw his hat hanging on a hook next to the door. He decided to place the hook at his eye level so he would be sure to look right at his hat on his way out. This way he would be sure to remember it. An umbrella hung from another hook right next to his hat. On the wall next to the door were three shelves. The lowest shelf held his computer. This area was wide enough for all the computer parts. The software and computer books were on a shelf above the computer. On the shelf above the books was a small stereo system. Mr. Conway sometimes enjoyed playing his radio or audio tapes while he worked. Next to these shelves was a small table where a slide projector was kept.

Across the room was a screen which Mr. Conway pulled down when he made slide presentations to his staff. A world map hung directly below the screen. The screen would cover the map when pulled down.

A four drawer file cabinet stood in the corner. A planter with three different plants was on top of the file cabinet. Mr. Conway enjoyed the plants. He waters them every week.

On this Friday afternoon all was in order. Mr. Conway walked over to the door, reached for his hat and switched off the lights before he left.

The following day Mr. Conway was in an auto accident and was almost killed. He recovered from most of his injuries, but was partly paralyzed and will probably never be able to walk again.

When he returned to his office things looked quite different to him from his wheel chair. He knew many changes would have to be made.

Write about or discuss the changes that must be made in order for Mr. Conway's office to, once again, be a convenient place for him to work. Describe how the office looks after the changes are made.

*Defining and Describing*

THINKING ABOUT HOW DIFFERENT AND UNIQUE ROOMS, HOMES, CLASSROOMS, AND SCHOOLS ARE REMINDS ME OF HOW DIFFERENT AND UNIQUE PEOPLE ARE. TAKE MY BEST FRIEND... MY BEST FRIEND AND I ARE AS DIFFERENT AS NIGHT AND DAY.

REALLY! THAT DIFFERENT? YOUR BEST FRIEND IS THE EXACT, COMPLETE OPPOSITE OF YOU! WHAT SPECIES IS THAT?

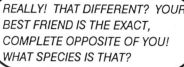

NO, WAIT A MINUTE. WE'RE NOT REALLY COMPLETELY, EXACTLY OPPOSITE - WE'RE JUST SORT OF DIFFERENT. "DIFFERENT AS NIGHT AND DAY" IS AN EXPRESSION WE USE WHEN WE COMPARE THINGS. REALLY IT'S JUST AN EXPRESSION NOT FOR REAL, VERY EXAGGERATED, BUT WE KNOW WHAT WE MEAN. SOMETIMES WE SAY THINGS LIKE THIS WHEN WE DESCRIBE.

YOU MEAN THEY'RE OTHERS?

YES. HERE ARE SOME OF THE EXPRESSIONS THAT HELP US DESCRIBE THINGS BY COMPARING. REMEMBER, MANY OF THESE COMPARISONS ARE EXAGGERATED, BUT WE USUALLY KNOW WHAT PEOPLE MEAN WHEN WE SAY THEM.

big as a house
black as coal
blind as a bat
blue as the sky
brave as a lion
brown as a berry
busy as a bee
clean as a whistle
clear as a bell
clear as crystal
clumsy as an ox
cold as ice
cool as a cucumber

cuddly as a kitten
cute as a button
dark as night
dead as a doornail
deep as the ocean
different as night and day
dry as a bone
easy as pie
fat as a pig
fit as a fiddle
flat as a pancake
free as a bird
fresh as a daisy

fresh as morning dew
gentle as a lamb
good as gold
green as grass
hairy as an ape
happy as a lark
hard as a rock
high as a kite
hungry as a bear
hungry as a wolf
light as a feather
like two peas in a pod
loud as thunder
mad as a hornet
mad as a wet hen
meek as a lamb
neat as a pin
old as the hills
pale as a ghost
playful as a kitten
pleased as punch
pretty as a picture
proud as a peacock
quick as a flash

quick as a wink
quiet as a mouse
red as a beet
sharp as a tack
sick as a dog
slippery as an eel
slow as a snail
sly as a fox
smart as a whip
smooth as silk
smooth as velvet
snug as a bug
stiff as a board
straight as an arrow
strong as an ox
stubborn as a mule
sweet as honey
thin as a rail
tough as leather
tough as nails
warm as toast
white as a sheet
white as snow
wicked as a witch
wise as an owl

*Defining and Describing*

Read each sentence. Think which of the exaggerated comparisons might describe the person in each sentence.

- Craig was in a hurry this morning. He had no time for breakfast and forgot his lunch. When he got home from school he was _____.

- Professor Horner is an expert in his field. He is often asked questions about events in the world. People know he will give the right answers. They say he is _____.

- Mr. Putner organizes everything very well. In his house there is a place for everything and everything is in its place. He is _____.

- The coach watched her players walk up to accept the championship trophy. She smiled a big smile and felt _____.

- The nurse was pleasant and kind. She slowly and carefully bandaged the child's injured leg, speaking softly telling him it would feel better soon. Because of her care the child relaxed and went to sleep. The nurse was _____.

- Pete bumped into the door, tripped over the rug and dropped the chair down the stairs while helping the family move. They were afraid he'd break the glass dishes and would not let him handle them. They said Pete was _____.

- Rodney ate six hot dogs, three ice cream cones, four candy bars and drank a large milk shake. Then he rode the merry-go-round and Ferris wheel. Suddenly he realized that all that food and activity was too much for him. He wanted to lie down because he felt _____.

- Jill was shocked and very upset when she saw that her house had been robbed. She stood staring at the empty rooms and her bright eyes became clouded and all the color drained from her face. She looked _____.

- Mr. Brown returned from the gym after his daily workout feeling healthy and ready to do some hard work. He works out and eats right and usually feels _____.

Can you think of animals which can be associated with these words?

aquatic_____

bivalve_____

bovine_____

canine_____

carnivorous_____

cold-blooded_____

cud-chewing_____

domestic_____

equine_____

feathered_____

feline_____

herbivorous_____

hoofed_____

horned_____

pachyderm_____

pedigreed_____

rabid_____

scaled_____

tame_____

tenacious_____

trained_____

univalve_____

venomous_____

warm-blooded_____

wild_____

winged_____

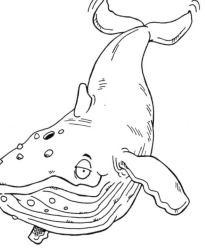

*Defining and Describing*

Here are some words that might be helpful in trying to describe foods.

a la carte
a la king
a la mode
appetizing
au gratin
baked
barbecued
bittersweet
blanched
braised
breaded
broiled
burnt
buttered

freeze dried
fresh brewed
frosted
frozen
glazed
grilled
high-fiber
home-cooked
home-grown
homogenized
instant

processed
raw
reduced-calorie
rich creamy
ripe
roast
roasted
sauteed
savory
scalloped
scrumptious
semi-sweet
sickening
smoked
smothered in
spoiled

candied
canned
carbonated
chiffon
cholesterol-free
chunky
country style
decaffeinated
deep fried
deep-dish
delicious
deluxe
deviled
effervescent
fat free
flat

iodized
jellied
light
low fat
luscious
marinaded
natural
nutritious
pickled
poached

stale
starchy
steamed
stewed
stuffed
succulent
sumptuous
sweet-and-sour
tantalizing
toasted
topped with
vitamin-enriched
whipped
whole grain
wholesome
zest

This should be fun! Pretend as though you are a famous chef. Create a special menu for a dinner party for your friends. Describe each selection.

---

# - - - MENU - - -

*Appetizer*

_____

_____

_____

*Main Course*

_____

_____

_____

_____

_____

*Dessert*

_____

_____

_____

*Beverage*

_____

_____

_____

---

*Defining and Describing*

Use these words when you describe various weather conditions.

blustering
breezy
bright
brisk
clear
cloudy
cold
cool
damp
dank
dewy
drafty
dreary
dry
foggy
freezing
frosty
gusty
hazy

hot
humid
inclement
misty
monsoon
muggy
nippy
overcast
shady
smoggy
stormy
sunny
torrid
tropical
turbulent
violent
warm
windy

Think about words associated with weather.

List some words that remind you of summer.

_____     _____     _____

_____     _____     _____

_____     _____     _____

List some words that remind you of winter.

_____     _____     _____

_____     _____     _____

_____     _____     _____

Pretend as though you're the weather reporter on your local TV station.

Prepare a favorable weather forecast.

_____

_____

_____

_____

_____

_____

Prepare an unfavorable forecast.

_____

_____

_____

_____

_____

_____

*Defining and Describing*

Sometimes when we describe things we associate them with a particular nation or culture.

| | | |
|---|---|---|
| African | European | Native American |
| American | French | Norwegian |
| Asian | German | Persian |
| Australian | Greek | Polish |
| Brazilian | Hawaiian | Puerto Rican |
| British | Indian | Russian |
| Cambodian | Irish | Scotch |
| Canadian | Italian | Slavic |
| Chinese | Jamaican | Spanish |
| Columbian | Japanese | Swedish |
| Danish | Jewish | Swiss |
| Dutch | Mexican | Turkish |
| English | | Vietnamese |

Think about the words which help us to associate things with particular nations or cultures. You've probably heard of some of these things or events. Can you guess with which culture each one is associated?

apple pie          _____

bagpipes           _____

baseball           _____

Big Ben            _____

Bolshoi Ballet     _____

bull fighter       _____

chop suey          _____

coffee             _____          muffins        _____

czar               _____          pastry         _____

Eiffel Tower       _____          polka          _____

elephant           _____          perfume        _____

guru               _____          pyramids       _____

hieroglyphics      _____          rodeo          _____

hula dance         _____          sauerkraut     _____

jazz               _____          shamrock       _____

Matzo balls        _____          shish kebob    _____

mounted police     _____          spaghetti      _____

                                             super bowl     _____

                                             sushi          _____

                                             taco           _____

                                             Taj Mahal      _____

                                             tea & crumpets _____

                                             the Vatican    _____

                                             Uncle Sam      _____

*Defining and Describing*

Here are some words that we use to describe actions.
These words are called *adverbs*.

accidentally
boldly
calmly
carefully
carelessly
cautiously
correctly
dangerously
deliberately
directly
easily
electrically
fiercely
gently
gracefully
happily
indirectly

lazily
leisurely
mechanically
merrily
mysteriously
neatly
nervously
noisily
perfectly
politely
powerfully
promptly
purposely
quickly
quietly
rapidly

readily
recklessly
regularly
roughly
sadly
safely
shakily
silently
slowly
suddenly
surely
swiftly
thoroughly
violently
wearily
wildly

Here's a challenge.  In the space below is a story where some of these adverbs are used.  The **blanks** have been filled in, but the **story** is missing!  Write a story using the words as they appear.  Have fun!

**Once upon a time** _____

_____

_____

_____. **Suddenly** _____

_____

_____

_____. **Cautiously** _____

_____

_____

_____ **Fiercely** _____

_____

_____ **courageously.** _____

_____

_____

_____ **slowly.** _____

_____

_____

**Boldly** _____

_____

_____

_____ **happily** _____.

*Defining and Describing*

*Defining and Describing* ©Circuit Publications

# NOTES

■ This book suggests that students might be more comfortable defining and describing objects and creatures if they had a format or structure to guide them. Students should be familiar with the item before they attempt to use the suggested formats; information should be derived from various sources including dictionaries. We encourage students to seek information about novel objects from a dictionary, to incorporate this with information from other sources and then formulate their own definitions and descriptions.

■ Page 91 offers suggestions for making definitions "a little easier." One of the suggestions calls attention to terms that can be used in place of words like *thing* and *stuff*. Another suggestion deals with defining complicated objects. In addition to these points, it is suggested that students who are having difficulty learning the names of classifications, be encouraged to substitute the use or function of an item in place of its category. This follows the natural course of development of defining. As children are learning to attend to and identify names of classifications they gradually replace terms denoting the use or function of an object with the name of its category.

■ On page 105 Mazey asks Charles to guess what she is defining by giving him a the name of the classification and a list of characteristics. She is actually defining an object that does not exist on this planet--something totally unfamiliar to Charles. It is then suggested that students make up definitions of objects or creatures that are equally unfamiliar. This exercise provides a chance to practice the *format* of a definition using imagination and having fun. This way students need not be concerned with accurately identifying an actual object.

■ Pages 117 to 122 direct attention to how descriptions change with different points of view. Some of the exercises actually suggest composing different descriptions while viewing a place from different points of view. Page 122 depicts an office from the point of view of someone before and after an accident confining him to a wheelchair. Such exercises might lead to growing understanding and expression of different points of view in a broader sense. As we try to introduce concepts of opposing views in government, social issues or political campaigns, it might be helpful to refer to activities such as describing a place from two or more positions. Pointing out a parallel between looking at the subject of a description and looking at a political issue from different points of view might help introduce debatable topics.

■ Finally, pages 138 and 139 are referred to as *generic worksheets*, one for defining and one for describing. The intent here is for the teacher to create describing and defining activities by asking students to define or describe terms which pertain specifically to particular lessons (social studies or science terms, field trip experiences, unique items used in special events, etc).

---

# REFERENCES

1.  Benilli, B. (1988). *On The Linguistic Origin of Superordinate Categorization*. Human Development. 31, 20-27.

2.  Bjorklund, D. and Jacobs, J.W. (1985). *Associative and Categorical Processes in Children's Memory: The Role of Automaticity in the Development of Organization in Free Recall*. Journal of Experimental Child Psychology. 39, 599-617.

3.  Haliday, M.A.K. and Hasan, R. (1976). *Cohesion in English*. London, Longman.

4.  Watson, R. (1985). Towards a Theory of Definition. *Journal of Child Language*. 12, 181-197.

5.  Wehren, A., De Lisi, R., and Arnold, M. (1981). The development of noun definition. *Journal of Child Language*. 1, 165-175.

---

When you **define** something give the
name of the object (or creature), the
name of its classification, and some
characteristics that make it special.

<u> name </u> is <u> classification </u> <u> characteristics </u> .
         **name of**

Define the following items using the lines below:

_____

_____

_____

_____

_____

_____

_____

_____

_____

_____

_____

_____

_____

_____

_____

_____

*Defining and Describing*

Use this list of hints to help you think of words to use when you are **describing** something.

Describe the following items using the lines below:

_____

_____

_____

_____

_____

_____

_____

_____

_____

_____

_____

_____

_____

_____

*TO DESCRIBE IS TO TELL OR WRITE ABOUT SOME-THING SO THAT YOUR LISTENER OR READER KNOWS EXACTLY HOW IT LOOKS, SOUNDS, SMELLS, TASTES OR FEELS.*

_____

_____

_____

_____

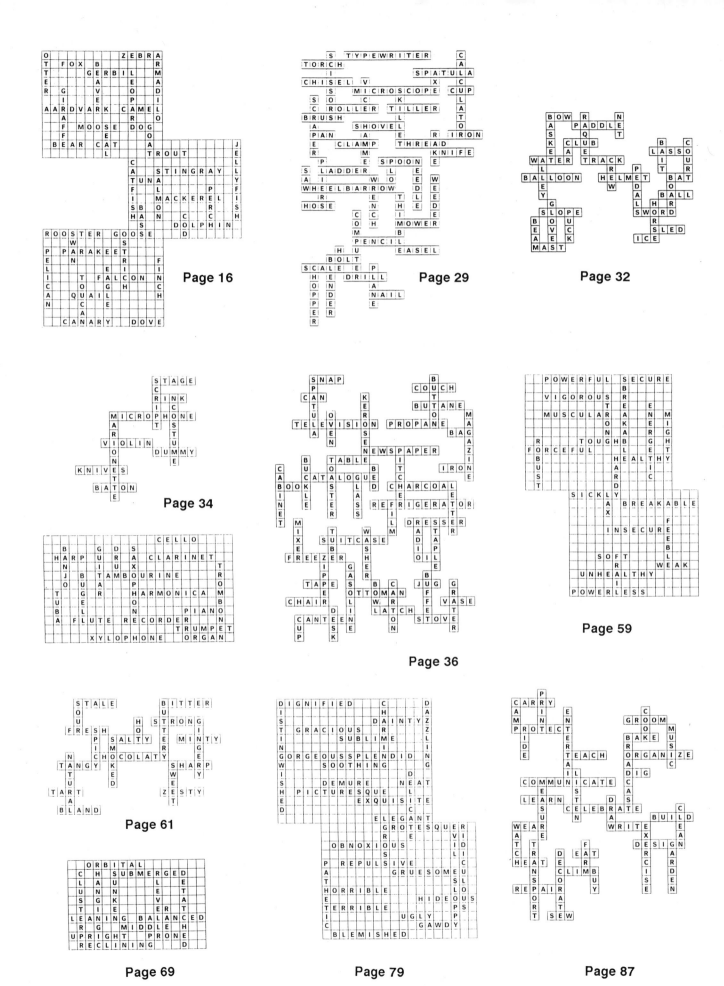

**Page 16**

**Page 29**

**Page 32**

**Page 34**

**Page 36**

**Page 59**

**Page 61**

**Page 69**

**Page 79**

**Page 87**

*Defining and Describing* ©Circuit Publications